# Dyeing &
# Printing

EXCALIBUR BOOKS

Edited by Thomas Browne

Published in the United States by
Excalibur Books
201 Park Avenue South
New York, New York 10003

First printing 1977

Printed in Great Britain

ISBN 0-525-70020-X

The chapter entitled 'Relief
printing' tells you how to
make pictures from found
objects—some as delicate as
this leaf. The variety of effects
that can be achieved is endless.

# Introduction

Here at last all the major techniques for decorating cloth and paper are found under a single cover. Whether you want to print your own matching wallpaper and curtains or just change the colour of some clothes, *Dyeing and Printing* tells you how. Had you ever thought of using linoleum to print dress patterns, or potatoes to make your own letterhead?

The intricacies of batik and tie-dyeing are unravelled and exotic crafts such as tritik and ikat are introduced. Using any of these related dyeing techniques you can produce original designs for dressmaking, curtains, bedspreads and cushions, and a variety of other uses in and around the home.

Screen printing is one of the most versatile ways of decorating either cloth or paper. It is very easy to make your own screen, and *Dyeing and Printing* gives straightforward guidance. Photographic stencils expand the scope of screen printing considerably and allow you to use designs and motifs from almost any source. Using light-sensitive emulsion you can produce photographic stencils in your own home and use them, for instance, to print personalized T-shirts for you or your family.

Having such an impressive array of crafts at your command allows you to choose the most suitable method for your needs. The numerous illustrations and diagrams not only help you to understand the techniques involved but are also packed with imaginative ideas. The final chapter—'Mixed-media printing'—shows how different crafts can be combined to good effect, but at the same time, each part of *Dyeing and Printing* stands on its own and you are at liberty to begin wherever you like.

# Contents

# Basic dyeing

# Basic dyeing techniques

| Present colour of article | Can be dyed |
|---|---|
| White | Any colour |
| Red | Maroon, deep brown, navy, purple, crimson |
| Pale green | Emerald, dark green, deep brown, navy |
| Dark green | Darker green |
| Yellow | Green, tangerine, red, navy, brown, maroon |
| Beige | Red, brown, deep brown, maroon, dark green, navy |
| Brown | Deep brown |
| Pale blue | Royal, navy, brown, deep brown, dark green |
| Royal blue | Navy |
| Any colour | Black |

Remember it is only possible to dye darker shades to lighter colours if the darker colours are first removed.

Some of the most attractive designs produced on cloth are those made by classic dyeing techniques such as batik, tie-dye and bleach dye. These are fascinating processes to work with but before you can undertake them and carry dyeing to its fullest expression you will need a grounding in dyeing principles – what dyes are, and what they will and won't do. To get to know and understand dyes you can start with the colours around you, transforming an old pink blouse into a vivid burnt orange or changing garish patterned curtains into subdued woodland shades.

## What dyes are

Dyes are colours produced either chemically or from plants, and are combined with a 'mordant' or fixing agent that enables them to penetrate the material being dyed. The most important point to remember about dye is that, unlike paint, it does not build up on the surface but is absorbed into the pores of the material. This means that if another colour is already present, the new dye will blend with it instead of covering it. So, while you can paint a blue wall yellow by adding enough coats, if you dye a blue curtain yellow, it will turn out green.

This does not mean, however, that you can never transform yellow curtains to blue – in many cases it is possible to strip out the old colour, leaving a neutral foundation for the new one – but it does mean that you should know what combinations of colours produce other colours. These are illustrated in the colour guide. Two kinds of dyes can be bought for home dyeing: hot- and cold-water dyes. A third type of dye, vat dye, is used commercially, especially for cottons and rayons, but because of the chemicals involved it is rarely used at home.

## Hot-water dyes

Hot-water dyes can be used on a variety of fabrics (see Fabric Chart) but since they require simmering, which means reaching a temperature of 82°-93°C (180°-200°F), it is wise to check the washing instructions on any garment you are dyeing. Although

6

many fabrics will take hot-water dye, they may themselves be damaged in the process.

Hot-water dye is available in both powder and liquid form. The powder must be mixed with boiling water before use, while the liquid is already mixed, and is more convenient for larger items since it contains more dye. Both require the addition of salt as a mordant. All brands of dye have instructions on the packet giving step-by-step directions for mixing the dye and completing the dyeing process. They usually state what weight of dry cloth a packet will dye.

Before you begin, therefore, it is necessary to weigh the dry fabric to find out how much dye you will need. To work properly, fabric must be thoroughly wet before immersion in the dye solution. The dyeing process itself involves simmering the cloth in the solution for a maximum of 20 minutes. If, halfway through the dyeing time, your fabric appears to have taken the new colour, don't be tempted to remove it as the full time is required for the colour to become fixed. It is possible, however, to lighten or darken the shade by leaving the cloth in for a longer or shorter time, but you should practise with a sample piece of cloth first. When the colouring has taken, remove the cloth from the container and rinse until the water runs clear, then wring or spin lightly and dry away from the sun or direct heat. (With wool, let the fabric cool before rinsing). If items are too large to fit into a container on a stove, you can dye them in a washing machine. Use a half-load capacity so the fabric can move freely inside and the dye can circulate throughout, otherwise the result will be patchy. Manufacturers' instructions include information about machine dyeing. Should you choose to use this process, make sure to clean the washing machine thoroughly when you have finished.

Among commercial dyes, hot-water dyes are the least colourfast and items should be washed separately since the colour tends to bleed into the rest of the wash. Over a period of time, hot-water dyes gradually lose their strength and garments may require re-dyeing. Items dyed in hot-water dyes can always be stripped, so if you don't like a colour or get tired of it you can change it.

## Cold-water dyes

Cold-water dyes are generally colour- and light-fast and are ideal for anything that has to be washed regularly. However, they only work on natural fibres (cotton, linen, wool and silk) and on viscose rayon. Being colour-fast, they cannot be stripped out.

Cold-water dye fabric has to be immersed for an hour but it is more convenient to use because once the dye is mixed you can dye in the

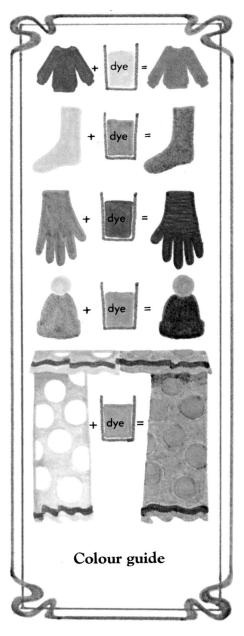

**Colour guide**

*Objects of one colour dyed another produce a third colour. Patterned curtains, when dyed another colour, produce a different colour combination.*

7

sink or bath tub. Always wear rubber gloves when using this dye as it is very hard to get off, especially from under nails and around cuticles. If you do stain your hands, wash them with diluted bleach and then dip them in vinegar.

If you are dyeing something large in the bath tub, remember that fabric can double its weight when wet and it may become too heavy to lift out and rinse. Add the dye solution to enough cold water to cover the fabric well. Add the recommended amount of salt (which makes the cloth receptive to the dye) and soda, if required, (to fix the dye), dissolving them in hot water first. (Wool needs different treatment, however. Instead of salt and soda, vinegar is added and warm water is used instead of cold.) When the fabric has been soaked for an hour, rinse it, wash in very hot water and washing powder, then rinse again until the water runs clear.

If you use a washing machine, follow the instructions on the

### Fabric chart

A risk is taken when immersing any fabric in a higher water temperature than that recommended in the washing instructions. Simmering, which hot-water dyes and stripping require, means immersing in a temperature of 82°-93°C (180°-200°F). No fabric can be stripped that has been vat dyed or cold-water dyed. (C=cold, H=hot dyes). The left hand column applies to the UK and the centre column to the US.

| | | |
|---|---|---|
| **Wool** (not cashmere, mohair, angora) **(C & H)**<br>**Cotton (C & H)**<br>**Linen (C & H)**<br>**Silk (C & H)** | **Wool** (not cashmere, mohair, angora) **(C & H)**<br>**Cotton (C & H)**<br>**Linen (C & H)**<br>**Silk (C & H)** | Cold water is gentler to fabrics since it doesn't require cooking and colours are faster. Special cold-water silk dyes are available, but are not colourfast. |
| **Rayon** (Evlan, Sarille) **(C & H)**<br>**Nylon** (Bri-nylon, Enkalon) **(H)**<br>**Acetates** (Dicel, Lansil) **(H)**<br>**Elastomerics** (Spanzelle, Lycra) **(H)**<br>**Triacetates** (Tricel, Arnel) **(H)** | **Rayon** (Avril, Zantrel) **(C & H)**<br>**Nylon** (Antron, Celonese, Enka) **(H)**<br>**Acetates** (Arnel, Celanese) **(H)**<br>**Spandex** (Lycra, Vyrene) **(H)**<br>**Triacetates** (Tricel, Arnel) **(H)** | |
| **Polyesters** (Terylene, Trevira, Tergal, Dacron, Crimplene) **(H)**<br>**Polyester/Nylon** (Helanka) **(H)** | **Polyesters** (Kodel, Fortrel, Vycrone, Dacron, Crimplene) **(H)**<br>**Polyester/Nylon** (Helanka) **(H)** | Dye to a paler shade of chosen colour. |
| **Polyester mixtures (H)**<br>**Glass Fibre and fabrics with special finishes**<br>(Permanently pleated, crease-resistant, flame- or dirt-proofed, bonded) | **Polyester mixtures (H)**<br>**Fibreglass and fabrics with special finishes**<br>(Permanently pleated, crease-resistant, flame- or dirt-proofed, bonded) | Cannot be stripped or dyed at home as they are non-porous. |
| **Acrylics** (Acrylan, Orlon, Courtelle, Dralon, Teklan, Leacril) | **Acrylics** (Acrilan, Orlon, Creslan, Zefkrome, Zeftran) | Cannot be stripped or dyed domestically. |

packet. The machine must be used in different stages as no machine has a long enough cold wash or rinse cycle. Since machines vary, many dye manufacturers recommend that you write to them for advice on your particular model. Clean the machine immediately after use by running it, empty, with hot water, washing powder and a cupful of bleach.

## Stripping colour

Before you dye will you need to strip down to neutral? Yes, if the colour you are using is lighter than the original colour of the cloth. Yes, if the new colour is one which, when mixed with the old one, will produce an unwanted third colour. No, if the new colour will blend with the old one to produce the shade you want: e.g. you can dye a yellow dress with pink dye if you want to get coral. Vat dyes and cold-water dyes cannot be stripped. A variety of proprietary colour removers exist, some of which also remove stains.

To discover if a fabric will strip, test a small piece first. Complete the test as directed on the container, because occasionally a colour appears to strip when the fabric is wet but colour returns when it dries. Small items must be simmered for about 10 minutes in stripping solution, cooled, given a lukewarm rinse and then washed thoroughly. A washing machine can be used to strip larger items and instructions are given on the bottle. Wool must be handled very carefully and allowed to cool before rinsing in lukewarm water. Then wash in warm water and rinse again. Never strip wool in a washing machine. With acetate rayon, do not allow the temperature of the water to rise above 60°C (140°F).

## Special problems

Stains and dirt will not be hidden by dye but will show through, so always first wash and remove any stains from the fabric to be dyed. Faded fabrics cause special problems, since the faded areas will take the dye with more intensity than the non-faded areas, giving a patchy result. In such cases it is advisable to try and strip all the old colour out first. Don't dye swimsuits if you often swim in a swimming pool as no domestic dye is fast to chlorine.

Patterned fabrics usually will not strip but they can sometimes be over-dyed with interesting results. The strongest colour in the pattern should generally be picked to emphasize the new shade. For example, with a red, yellow and pale green pattern, you should use a red dye. The red will stay red, the yellow will turn orange and the pale green will become brown.

If you don't want red, you could use a blue dye to turn the red purple the yellow into green and the pale green into greeny-blue.

*Skeins of newly-dyed wool hang up to dry in the souk of Marakesh, the capital city of Morocco.*
*Dying is an ancient craft, found in every part of the world, and despite modern advances, the fundamental process remains the same.*

Before you start to dye an item, make sure you know what the fibre is. Fibreglass and many synthetics will not dye. Other fabrics need the dye most suitable for their particular kind of fibre. Also make sure the lining is a type of cloth that can be processed before you decide to dye or strip a lined item.

If the lining is a different colour from the main fabric, as is often the case with curtains, for example, then you must remember that the lining will dye a different colour, depending on its original shade.

## Effects with different dyes

Modern hot- and cold-water dyes make it possible to experiment with colour – not only on fabrics but on unusual materials like suede and surfaces such as fabric-covered shoes and handbags. These can be made darker in tone or changed into entirely different colours with very little effort. Of course, as with everything, a little practice helps. So don't throw your suede coat into a dye bath without trying to dye suede in a small way first. Begin with something you can afford to make a mistake on until you become familiar with the way each type of material takes dye. As your technique develops, you can try more and more imaginative ways to create original effects.

*Ordinary dyes can be painted on with a brush, once a thickening agent has been added, but special paint-on dyes are now also available.*

## Layering

This is just one way to achieve an eyecatching effect: try it with a long, flowing dress, a flared skirt, scarf or T-shirt – even tights. It's surprisingly simple to do yet looks like the result of a highly complicated process.

Wash your garment and soak it in the dye bath. Almost immediately begin to pull the garment out of the dye bath in stages – just a little at a time – but leave a small amount at the bottom in the dye for the full dyeing period. The result will be a delicate shading from pale to deep, rich tones in whatever colour you choose.

Layered effects are quicker to achieve with hot-water dyes but cold-water dyes (for natural fibres, viscose rayon) are completely colourfast, although they take longer. Macramé chokers and belts can also be given this clever touch. Mark the centre of the length of cloth. Then, starting at the middle and using cold-water dye, remove the item from the dye a little at a time at 15 minute intervals, leaving the ends in for a full hour. Always wash items afterwards to get rid of excess dye.

## Painting with dye

Special dye-thickening agents are available which are designed for painting with dye on fabric. Using this technique clothes can be given a totally original look, and no special artistic skill is necessary if you work from traced designs or use stencils. Wool takes the colour in a softer shade and painting on cotton/polyester mixtures gives a stippled effect that can be fascinating.

Wash and dry the garment first (if it is washable), then lay it out flat on a working surface which has been covered with old material or a plastic sheet. Mark out your design in pencil and then clip a piece of cardboard between the layers of fabric so that only the top layer takes the paint. Mix cold dye, thickening agent and fixative. Together they make a gel which you paint onto the fabric with a stiff brush. Apply more thickly for deeper colour. The gel looks like a paint but acts like a dye because, if painted over a colour, it combines with that colour to produce a third.

The fabric actually dyes as it dries. So leave the fabric to dry naturally for about six hours, then scrub off the thickener with cold water. Wash and iron the material in the usual way for the fabric to regain its natural feel: the colours are absolutely fast when dry.

## Fabric shoes and handbags

Satin, crepe or canvas shoes and handbags can be dyed to match or tone with your outfit simply by making up the required dye solution and stroking it on smoothly with a soft toothbrush. Use hot-water dye for satin and crepe, and cold-water dye for canvas. Before dyeing, pad out the fronts of shoes first with paper or rags and wet the fabric thoroughly. The edges of the soles can be masked with tape.

## Dyeing suede

It is sometimes difficult to buy suede in exactly the shade you want as most items come in a limited colour range. Dyes enlarge the possibilities for suede garments and accessories and are invaluable for reviving old suede or decorating it with dyed appliqués of suede flowers or patchwork. There are special suede dyes which, unlike leather paints, are true dyes and react with the original colour to form a third. For example, if you dye a pair of red shoes with blue dye they will end up as purple. It's always better to dye light tones to a darker colour or to freshen them with their own colour. Suede stays supple even after several coats of dye.

Make absolutely sure that all grease and dust is removed first, then brush the surface to bring up the nap. Apply the colour to a small area at a time, working the dye well in with the brush provided. Leave the suede to dry thoroughly, brush to bring up the nap again, then apply a second coat and brush again when dry.

*The shaded effect of the dress is produced by dyeing in stages. The scarf is coloured with paint-on dye.*

11

# Home-made dyes

All around us, in the town, in the country and even in the kitchen, we are surrounded by plants which make dyes and which, according to the various methods of dyeing, give a fascinating variety of hues. The principle of plant dyeing is simply to extract dye by simmering a large quantity of the plant – flowers, berries, leaves or bark – in water. It is an ancient art, and people in many different parts of the world still produce wonderful variations of colour from the plants around them. The rich shades that characterize Persian rugs and carpets, for example, come from vegetable dyes which with age develop a softness of colour unlike anything produced with modern commercial dyes.

Dyeing from plants is fun and it is basically easy to do, but you need a willingness to experiment to get the most enjoyment out of it because no two plants are ever quite the same and they can give surprising results. How simple the plants you need are to obtain depends largely on where you live and what season it is. Madder and indigo may be difficult to find but onions and turmeric can be purchased locally. However, for anyone really interested in natural dyeing it makes sense to grow your own dye plants. Many, such as onions and dahlias, are easily cultivated.

## Fabrics

Wool is the best material for vegetable dyeing. Cotton, silk and linen can be dyed, but they usually require rather complicated processes and so are not dealt with here. Yarn is particularly suitable because hanks of it can be dyed with different plants, depending on the amount of dyestuff available, and then knitted or crocheted into clothes of one or more colours. Any white, woolen garment can be dyed, and those which are beginning to yellow will take on new life when dyed a colour from nature.

## Equipment

Apart from dyestuffs and mordants, you need no more equipment than what can be found in any kitchen. As long as you are sure that the plants you are using are not poisonous you can use your

cooking pans and sieve, provided they are large enough. But if you intend to experiment with new dyes, do not use your cooking utensils for dyeing. You will also need rubber gloves and a stick for stirring; an old mop handle will do or, if you prefer, a wooden dowel or a glass rod. If you are dyeing several colours, you will need a different stick for each one.

## Extracting dyes

Colour is extracted from plants by simmering, preferably in soft rain-water. If this is not available then soften tap water with a water softener. Extracting dye can take anything from 20 minutes to three hours, depending on the plant or the part of the plant you are using. As a general rule, tender sections, such as flowers and leaves, need less simmering and will become dull if cooked too long, while tougher sections, such as hard berries and barks, may need pounding beforehand and require longer cooking to draw out their colour.

Plant dyeing is more of an adventure than a science and it is impossible to predict the exact shade a colour will take, since plants vary with the season and the locality. One way to get an idea of the strength and colour of your dye is to immerse a sample piece of yarn with the plant. Considerable quantities may often be needed to produce dyes; the amount varies with each plant, but 113gm (4oz) of plant material to 28gm (1oz) of wool is a useful guideline.

To extract dye, cover the plant material with soft water and keep adding more hot water as it simmers. When the dye has been extracted, strain off the liquor. You can throw the plant remains onto a compost heap. Let the liquor cool to body temperature before you add the wool. Dyes can be stored for future use in tightly sealed jars and kept in a refrigerator.

## Direct dyeing

There are two ways to dye wool – by direct dyeing and by mordant dyeing. A mordant is a chemical which has an affinity for both fibres and dyestuffs and which improves both the colour and the fastness of the dye. Not many plants can dye direct, i.e. without a mordant to fix the colour. Those which can include onion skins, sloe berries, bilberries [blue berries], black walnut shells, white snowberry (*symphoricarpos albus*), common grey wall lichen, turmeric, golden-rod and ragwort.

To dye direct, first wet the wool thoroughly. If you are dyeing an old garment it is wise to wash it to make sure it is clean and receptive to the dye. Hanks of yarn can be tied very loosely and put

---

**Brown**
Big Bud Hickory – bark (Carya tomentosa)
Black Walnut – hulls (Juglans nigra or J. regia)
Cutch – heart wood of tree and the pods (Acacia species)
Grey Lichen – whole plant (Parmelia saxatilis)
Larch – needles (Larix species)
Mahogany wood chips or sawdust
Mountain Laurel – leaves (Kalmia latifolia)
Oak – bark (Quercus species)
Pyracantha – twigs (Pyracantha angustifolia)

**Orange**
Coreopsis – flowers (Coreopsis tinctoria or C. marmorata)
Dahlia – orange flowers (Dahlia species)
Lady's Bedstraw – roots (Galium boreale or G. verum)
Madder – roots (Rubia tinctorum)
Onion – outer skins (Allium cepa)

straight into the dye-bath, but balls of yarn will not dye right through and must be rewound in some looser way.

Put the wet wool into the dyebath and raise the temperature very slowly to simmering point. Keep the dyebath simmering for the time required to get the depth of colour you want. This can vary a great deal; some dyes, such as onion skins and turmeric, 'take' very quickly, while black walnut shells require up to three hours. Never allow the dyebath to boil vigorously as this can destroy the colour and may cause the woolen fibres to matt.

While the wool is simmering, stir it occasionally to make sure the dye is reaching all parts of the material. Use a glass or wooden stick and from time to time lift the wool up to check the intensity of the colour. When deciding if the correct intensity has been reached, bear in mind that the colour will be somewhat lighter when the wool is dry.

When the colour is deep enough, let the wool drip over the pan for a minute. Then, wearing rubber gloves, squeeze each hank lightly and plunge it into warm, soft water. Rinse thoroughly—it is very important to rinse out all the surplus dye or the cloth will bleed later when it is washed. Always dry wool in a cool, shady place.

## Mordant dyeing

There are many substances which act as mordants to improve the colour and fastness of dyes, but two of the best known are alum and iron, obtainable from pharmacies. Alum generally has the effect of brightening natural dyes while fixing the colour at the same time. Iron also fixes colour, but has the effect of darkening it and, in the case of many yellow dyes, turning them to green.

To mordant with alum (potassium aluminium sulphate – available from pharmacies), use 28gm (1oz) or $1\frac{3}{4}$ teaspoons of alum for each 113gm (4oz) of wool. Mordanting is usually done before dyeing. Stir the alum well into enough soft water to cover the wool and allow it to move easily in a container. Add the wet wool. In the case of yarn, always tie the hanks loosely to prevent them from tangling. Heat the vessel slowly, taking about an hour to reach simmering point, and keep it simmering gently for another hour, moving the wool from time to time with a stirring rod. Then let the water cool until the wool can be handled. Let it drip over the pot, then squeeze gently but do not wring or rinse. Dye the wool immediately, or dry it in a towel and store it.

It is possible to mordant with alum at the same time as you are dyeing by adding alum directly to the dyebath, but there is a greater chance the wool may dye unevenly. Also, since mordanting with alum takes some time, it is advisable to mordant as much wool at

---

**Rose. pink. purple**
Bilberry – fruits (Vaccinium species)
Black currant – fruits (Ribes nigrum)
Black Huckleberry – fruits (Gaylussacia baccata)
Blackberry – fruits (Rubus species)
Elder – fruits (Sambucus nigra and S. canadensis)
Sloe – fruits (Prunus spinosa)
Wild Grape Vine – grapes (Vitis species)

**Red**
Bloodroot – roots (Sanguinaria canadensis)
Dahlia – red flowers (Dahlia species)
Geranium – red flowers (Pelargonium species)
Hemlock Tree – bark (Tsuga species)
Lady's Bedstraw – roots (Galium boreale or G. verum)
Madder – roots (Rubia tinctorum)
Pokeweed – berries (Phytolacca americana)
Prickly-Pear Cactus – fruity protuberances (Opuntia polycantha)

one time as you can manage. Mordanted wool can be stored in bags containing moth repellent and taken out as needed.

To mordant with iron (ferrous sulphate, also known as copperas and green vitriol), add the iron to the dyebath in the last 15 to 30 minutes of dyeing. Always lift the wool out before stirring in the mordant, then replace it and let it simmer again. This will result in a deeper, and somewhat darker, tone. Use very little iron – about 4gm ($\frac{1}{8}$oz), just under a teaspoon, to 113gm (4oz) of wool. Too much iron tends to make wool rough. Iron rust or iron filings can be used for mordanting, but they need greater quantities to be effective. Always remember to rinse well in warm water after dyeing to retain the softness of the wool.

## Recipes for dyes

There are innumerable recipes for plant dyeing and the dye charts show some of the colours which different plants produce. These can all be varied by the addition of mordants and by other subtle changes in dyeing time and treatment. Amateur dyers are constantly finding new colours which can be worked together in embroidery, crochet and weaving, and this is part of the fun of plant dyeing. To find out if a new plant can be used as a dye, put in a small piece of yarn to simmer with the plant.

**Yellow** Onion skins, ragwort, golden-rod and turmeric powder all dye yellow and can be used to dye direct or mordanted with alum for additional vividness and colour fastness. Onion and turmeric 'take' very fast and after several minutes the yarn will turn a pale yellow. A deeper hue develops in 20 to 40 minutes. The long-johns hanging on the clothes-line in the photograph were dyed with onion skins. The skins were simmered for one hour and the long-johns for 40 minutes, with alum in the dyebath.

**Green** Proceed as above to dye yellow. Then lift the yellow wool out of the dyebath and add iron mordant, 4gm ($\frac{1}{8}$oz) per 113gm (4oz) of wool. Put the dyed wool back in to simmer again until it turns green. Different skeins lifted out at different times will emerge in a variety of green shades.

**Red** Madder is the easiest red dye to use, and can either be bought or extracted by simmering the dried outer skins of the root. The red shirt in the picture was dyed with madder. Mordant wool with alum and simmer in the dyebath for an hour, keeping the temperature below 60°C (140°F). If the temperature is too high the colour will go orange in tone.

**Brown** To extract dye, simmer walnut shells for three hours, then direct-dye wool by simmering from one to three hours, depending on how dark a shade you want.

---

**Green**
Bracken – young tops (Pteridium aquilinum)
Fustic – wood as chips (Chlorophora tinctoria)
Golden-rod – tops with flowers (Solidago species)
Horsetail – green above ground part (Equisetum species)
Ivy – berries when black (Hedera helix)
Lily of the Valley – leaves (Convallaria majalis)
Nettle – leaves and tops (Urtica dioica)
Privet – leaves (Ligustrum vulgare)
Weld – leaves and tops (Reseda luteola)

**Black or grey**
Alder – bark (Alnus species)
Blackberry – young tips (Rubus species)
Buckthorn – berries (Rhamnus caroliniana, R. cathartica)
Butternut – nuts (Juglans cinerea)
Logwood – bark (Haematoxylon campechianum)
Yellow Flag Iris – roots (Iris pseudacorus)

# Dyeing yarn many colours

With even the simplest random dyeing of yarn, extraordinary abstract patterns emerge when the yarn is knitted up. Watching them develop adds a new interest to knitting; the pattern of colours is constantly changing, especially as stitches are added and dropped to fashion the contours of a garment. Multi-coloured yarn can also be used in weaving to create random effects or to produce a repeated feathery pattern. Yarn can be random dyed in slightly different ways depending on the number of colours and the frequency of colour change desired, but all the skeins needed to complete the article you wish to knit or weave must be dyed at the same time to ensure uniformity of tones.

While commercial hot- and cold-water dyes are perfectly suitable for random dyeing, natural dyes should also be considered. These have especially rich and subtle tones and although much plant material is normally needed for making natural dyestuffs small quantities can make enough dye for random effects.

Random dyeing is a good way to use up odd balls of wool, and although white is the best colour to work with, other colours can be re-dyed provided you have a basic knowledge of how dyes blend: for example, that blue over-dyed yellow produces green but over-dyed with orange it produces rust. Another possibility is to remove the old colour with a proprietary dye-remover.

## Space dyeing

The simplest process for dyeing yarn in several colours is by space dyeing. This involves 'spacing' the colours along a hank of yarn. An easy introduction to space dyeing is to use two colours and leave part of the yarn white. This is particularly effective for pale shades such as those used on baby clothes or feminine knitwear.

Prepare two dye vats according to manufacturer's instructions (or using natural dyes). Divide the skein of yarn into three equal sections and tie two cords loosely round as a marker (fig.1). Wet the skein and dip it into a dye vat. You can put one end in each vat if the vats are close together; otherwise dye one end and then the other. Finally, squeeze each dyed section gently to remove

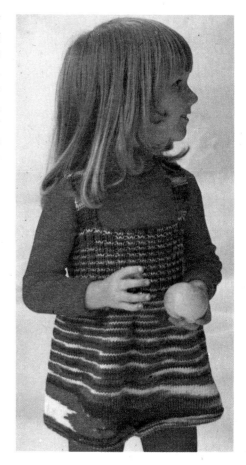

*The colourful striped design of this knitted dress is the result of using random-dyed woolen yarn – an unpredictable pattern emerges as you knit the garment.*

excess water, rinse thoroughly and allow the skein to dry. Dyed areas can be shaded by varying the amount of time the yarn remains in the dye-bath. Shading will also occur where the dye bleeds into the white. 'Blended' space dyeing involves overlapping some of the dyed areas so that new colours result and a knowledge of the shades produced by the various combinations of colours is necessary.

This technique produces a more variegated effect as many more colours can be produced from the same number of dyes. A rainbow effect, for example, can be achieved by the judicious mixing of the three primary colours: red, yellow and blue.

To make six colours using three, divide yarn into three sections as shown (fig.1) and tie loosely. Prepare three dye vats, one for each colour. Then dip one section in dye for the length of time required, then rinse thoroughly and squeeze gently to remove excess water. Now dye the second section but allow a small amount of the previous dyed section to be re-dyed in the new colour (fig.2). Rinse and squeeze the freshly dyed section then dye the third section in the same way, allowing ends of previously dyed sections to be re-dyed. This will result in three large areas of primary colour interspersed with three short sections of blended colour – in the case of red, yellow and blue the blended colours would be orange, green and purple (fig.3).

*1. The yarn is tied in a loop by loop knots in order to give greater control of the dyeing process. The knots also serve as markers between the various areas of colours.*

*2. Here the second section is being dyed yellow, and orange is produced where the yellow and red combine.*

*3. Random dyeing using the three primary colours produces an attractive rainbow effect.*

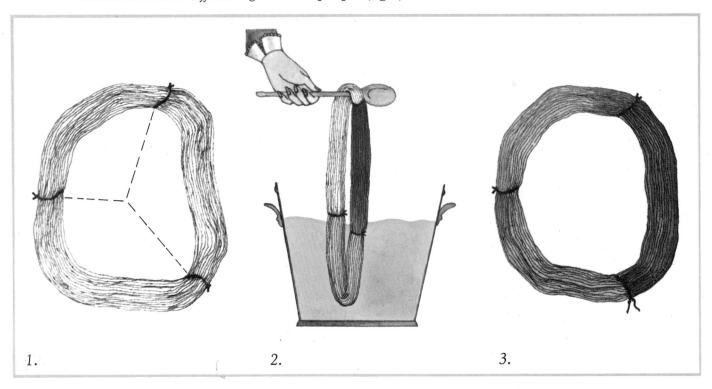

1.                    2.                    3.

# Tie-dyeing

# Introduction to tie-dyeing

Tie-dyeing is a way of decorating cloth by blocking out certain parts so that they do not 'take' the dye in which the cloth is dipped. This is done by knotting, folding, clipping, tying or binding the cloth so that the dye cannot penetrate these areas. Using tie-dye methods, you can create an array of patterns that have an extraordinarily illusory quality which is quite unlike anything else that printing or dyeing can produce. By planning which areas of the fabric you want to resist the dye, you can create repeated patterns, or position a large motif – such as a flamboyant sunburst – in the centre of a garment or any other object.

Tie-dyeing is an age-old craft which originated in the East, probably in China, and spread along the ancient routes of the silk caravans to many other lands. Medieval Japanese nobles dressed in tie-dyed silks, and in India and Indonesia the craft became a highly developed and refined form of decoration. Pre-Columbian examples of tie-dyeing have also been found in the Americas, and the craft is still practised extensively in Africa where a distinctive style of wonderfully bold patterns has arisen, often using indigo dyes.

## What will dye

Any fabric which is not too bulky can be tie-dyed as long as the fibre is receptive to dye. Silk is particularly beautiful when tie-dyed as its floating quality seems to lend itself to the radiant patterns which tie-dye produces. Cotton is perhaps the easiest fabric to work with because it takes dye extremely well and, being comparatively inexpensive, is a good choice for beginners. Natural fibres (cotton, linen, silk, wool) and viscose rayon can be dyed with commercial cold-water dyes. These are fibre-reactive dyes, which means that the dye molecules form a bond with the fibre, making it colourfast. Many synthetic fibres can be dyed with commercial hot-water dyes and these come in a wide range of colours and shades. Unfortunately, these dyes are not colourfast and must always be washed separately. Polyesters and fabrics with special finishes cannot be dyed.

Cloth that is going to be dyed must always be washed first to get rid

*The colourful pattern of these matching sheets and pillowcases was produced by bundling the linen into sausage shapes, tying it at random and dyeing it in a washing machine.*

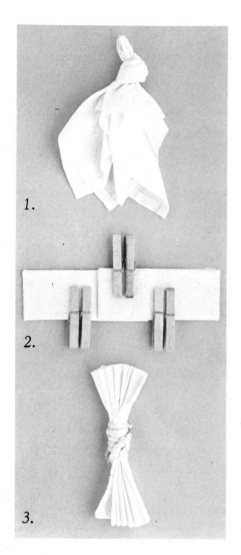

of any substance which may have been added by the manufacturer to give it 'body' and finish. Otherwise, the finish will prevent dye penetrating the cloth.

## Tying

Before you begin to tie the cloth it must be dry and free from creases. It is wise to experiment with a few squares of inexpensive cotton or strips of old sheets to find out about different effects, to try out different types of string and to see how tightly cloth should be bound to produce the desired effect.

All types of string will prevent penetration of the dye to some degree, but some strings will let dye penetrate more than others. Nylon string is totally resistant to cold-water dyes, fishing line, plastic cord, rope and linen thread can all be used effectively.

Cotton thread is receptive to dyes of all kinds and is therefore not suitable unless your fabric is thickly bunched or folded. With thick bunching you can make graded patterns of colour because the inner sections of cloth will receive little or no dye while the outer layers may receive some colour through the thread.

Resist objects of all sorts can be used in tie-dyeing to give interesting and unusual patterns, and you will be able to find many ordinary household items to use. Paper clips, clothes pegs (pins), bulldog clips, pipe cleaners – anything that grips the fabric, keeps dye out and is not itself harmed in the dyebath, will work and also will leave its own special mark or pattern. Rubber bands, wire, dental floss and masking tape are all useful substitutes for string. Several different objects can be combined to make a pattern on one piece of cloth and this is where your own ingenuity comes in. In the beginning you will have to test the result of each 'tie' before using it as a pattern, but as soon as you become familiar with the effects different ties produce, you can then visualize a pattern and carry it out.

Always consider which ties are most suitable for the type and weight of your material and for the use it will be put to. Fine cottons and silk, for instance, respond to fine threads and a close repetition of delicate ties, while fabrics of a looser weave need a large effect from knotting or clothes pegs. Repeated patterns should be marked with a pencil before tying begins, so that you can be sure of a regular repeat.

All string, thread or cord must be tied very, very tightly and knotted firmly, so that it does not loosen in the dyebath. If the string is unusually thick, or if for any reason there is a problem in getting the end of the string back to the beginning to make a knot, you can stitch the ends to the rest of the cord.

*Above and overleaf are shown some of the most useful 'ties' while the results they produce are shown opposite.*
*1. The simplest tie of all is a knot tied in the material.*
*2. Clothes pegs make interesting rectangular shapes. The cloth should be folded in accordion pleats for a repeated pattern.*
*3. Fold the cloth in half, accordion pleat it and then bind it with strong twine.*

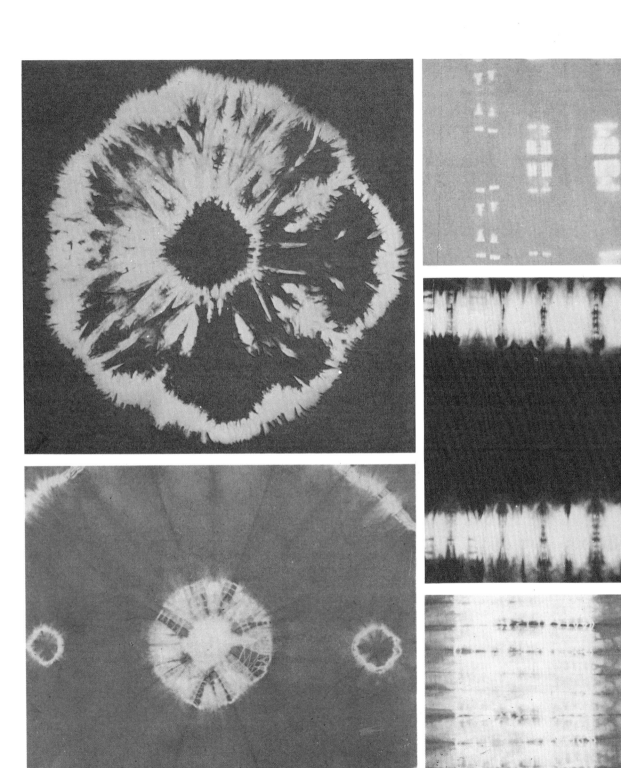

## Dyeing

When your ties are all securely knotted or fastened, wet the cloth thoroughly and put it into the dyebath for the length of time stated in the manufacturer's instructions. When the dye has taken, remove the fabric, leaving the ties intact, and rinse it thoroughly. If you have been using a hot-water dye it is advisable to give it a good wash before untying to get rid of any excess dye. Do not undo the ties until the cloth has had time to dry thoroughly, or dye may seep into the white, unprotected areas. When undoing the ties it is very easy to nip the cloth accidentally with your scissors, so be very careful and insert the point of the scissors under the end, not the middle, of the tie.

Special effects can be created with dyes by dipping only part of the cloth into the dye – along the edges of accordion folds, for example. Another fascinating effect comes from using bleach on cloth that has been dyed first, and then tied. This is a kind of reverse procedure because it is the dyed areas which make the pattern as the bleach removes the dye from the exposed areas. By tying cloth with thread or cord that has been dyed with a hot-water dye you can make coloured lines on fabric where the dye from the cord seeps through. Although it is much better to experiment on white cloth, you can begin with a light-coloured cloth, tie it, and dye a darker shade.

Some marvelous colour combinations can be made by using more than one dyebath. In this way, the second colour can be applied either before or after you undo the first ties. If you make more ties in the same cloth, without untying the first ones, and then put the cloth in a second dyebath, your first ties will result in a white pattern, your second ties will have the colour of the first dyebath, and the cloth which was exposed throughout will either be the colour of the last dyebath or a blend of both colours—when working with more than one colour it is very important to remember that dyes blend.

## Ikat

Ikat is derived from the Malaysian word 'mengikat' meaning 'to tie' and while the term generally refers to an ancient tie-dyeing technique associated with woven cloth, ikat or tie-dyed yarn can be used for knitting as well. With ikat-dyed yarn, a greater control of multi-dyed areas is possible since any number of sections can be bound off and therefore many shorter lengths of one colour can be produced. Ikat also facilitates control of dyed shades and neighbouring colours.

Yarn can be bound with almost anything that will not be harmed in

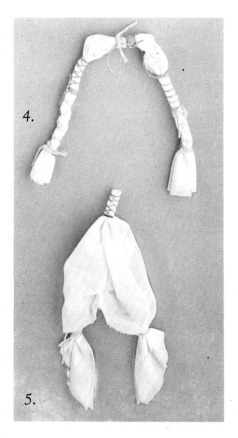

*4. First pleat the cloth as in fig.3 and then bind it tightly in a spiral pattern.*

*5. Cobweb-like circles can be produced by picking up the centre of the cloth with a needle, letting it fall in even folds, then binding the centre, inverting it and binding it again in a lump underneath.*

*Left: This huge shawl, which can also be used as a blanket or wall hanging, is a fine example of the ancient art of ikat.*

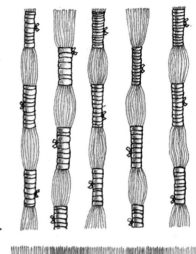

6.

7.

the dye-bath but will keep dye from penetrating the areas which are masked off. By binding off several areas, dyeing, rinsing, then binding off some more and dyeing the yarn again, three colours can be produced at required intervals on each skein.

Ikat weaving normally involves using multi-coloured yarn for either the warp or the weft but rarely for both. The effect of weaving the plain and the multi-colour together gives the soft, feathery quality characteristic of ikat. Yarn can also be used to produce a regular woven pattern such as a chessboard (fig.7), by dyeing predetermined sections for the loom.

6. *To tie-dye yarn for weaving, lay out the warp on a flat surface and then bind it as shown, masking the sections you do not wish to be dyed.*
7. *This orange chessboard pattern is the result of dipping bound yellow yarn in red dye.*

# Resist dyeing and tritik

Tying fabric with cords and clips to resist dye in the dyebath is by no means the only way to produce the radiant patterns that make tie-dyeing unique. Since medieval times the search for new and intricate patterns has produced many variations, and some of the oldest techniques are among the most sophisticated. These involve tying objects into cloth to make circular patterns or 'auroras' of different sizes, while 'tritik' involves stitching and then gathering the cloth to make fascinating designs caused by the inability of the dye to seep through the gathers.

## Tie-dyeing with objects

Many objects near at hand can be inserted into cloth 'pockets' to make effective tie-dyed designs – pebbles, corks, short lengths of match-sticks, beads, buttons, nuts and bolts and other miscellaneous bits of hardware all make useful tools for beginners to work with. The most beautiful tie-dye patterns made with objects, however, are obtained from the more demanding method of tying tiny pebbles into cloth to produce delicate all-over patterns.

Start with sizeable objects first. Place a tin can or glass ashtray in the centre of a piece of cloth, then bunch the fabric around the object to make a 'pocket' (fig.1). Tie the thread firmly around the bunched cloth and tie the two ends together in a strong knot. Then tie other random objects of different sizes and shapes at various distances from the the central object. It is important to realize that the purpose of the inserted objects is not to keep the dye from penetrating but to make a pucker which will affect the size and regularity of the pattern produced by the cord. When all your objects have been tied into the cloth, wet it thoroughly and place it in the dye-bath, following the manufacturer's instructions.

## Design

Once you get some idea of the effect produced by fairly large objects tied at random, you can plan a more careful piece of work by measuring out and marking with tailor's chalk the position of the 'inserts'. Different objects will, of course, make different sized

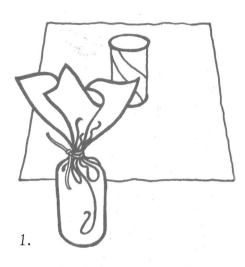

1.

*To bind objects into cloth, place them on the material one at a time, bunch the cloth up to make a pocket and tie the neck tightly.*

Small objects such as peas, pebbles or buttons tied into cloth will produce regular or irregular patterns depending on the way you lay them out.

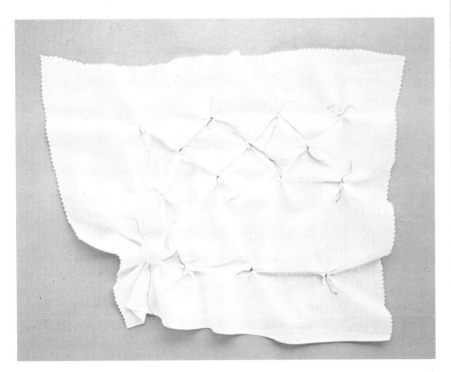

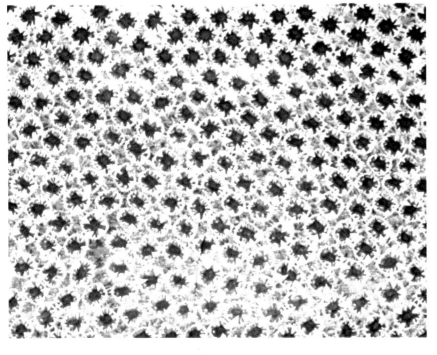

This tie-dyed cloth from Nigeria is designed to be worn as a turban or a flowing full-length garment. The pattern was produced by tying hundreds of tiny grains into the cloth before dyeing.

circles or ovals, but by tying objects at regular intervals a repeated pattern builds up. The tinier the objects the more closely they can be spaced and the more delicate will be the result. If objects are not spherical, the direction in which they are tied can also be important. Especially interesting effects can be obtained by alternating the direction of grains of long-grain rice, for instance.

In order to tie tiny objects tightly, it is a good idea to thread a darning or crewel needle and take a back stitch to start, leaving an end hanging. Then gather and wind the thread around the bunched cloth several times, pull it tight and tie the ends together. When the cloth has been dyed, dried and untied, the effect will be small blurred circles or stars which give an impression of sparkling. Sometimes, in delicately repeated patterns, the thread is carried from one tie to the next without cutting so that, when dyed, a fine line connects the tiny dots of the pattern.

Coloured objects can be inserted into the ties so as to yield up their colour to the cloth while it is being dyed another colour. Walnut shells, for instance, will produce a brown colour when simmered; bilberries, and various other berries will also produce colour. Tissue paper, felt and objects that are not colourfast can also be used in this way in a simmering dyebath.

## Tritik

The purpose of tritik (stitching) is the same as all tie-dyeing – to make a pattern by resisting the dye in which the cloth is put. This is done by making a row of stitches, and then pulling the thread to gather the cloth as tightly as possible. In tritik it is the folds or gathers rather than the thread that prevents the dye from getting through and so makes a pattern, but your choice of thread can also affect the process.

The running stitches used in tritik can be as small or as large as you choose, but as a general rule finer stitches should be used for more delicate motifs. Thread must be reasonably fine to prevent holes being made in the fabric when the thread is later pulled out, but it should also be strong enough not to break when it is pulled tight. Linen carpet thread or buttonhole thread, white linen sewing thread or even doubled sewing threads can all be used because it is the folds which provide the principal resistance, not the thread.

Begin to sew by making a small back stitch but leave a few inches of the end hanging. This will make it easier to gather the cloth and also secure the end (fig.2). When you have stitched the desired length of running stitch, be sure to finish on the same side of the cloth as you began. Now pull up the cloth as tight as possible and tie the ends of the thread in a strong knot. You are now ready for the dye bath.

*Begin to sew with a backstitch. Leaving a tail makes the stitch easier to tighten and tie off.*

2.

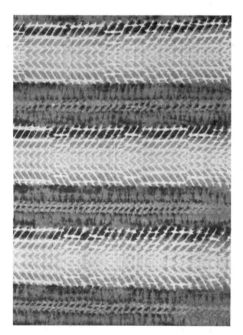

*The tied-dyed patterns on this cotton cloth were made by sewing overlapping rows of stitches.*

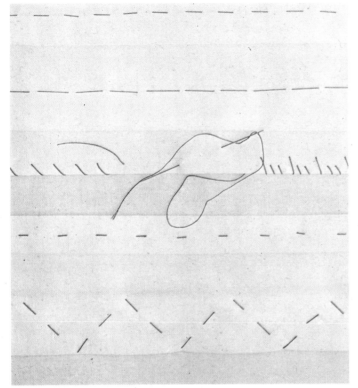
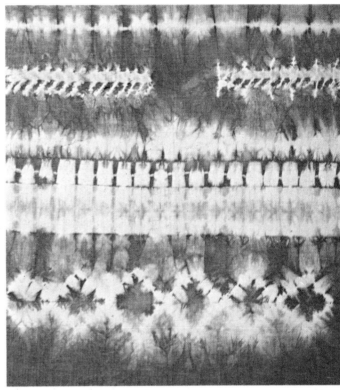

Always wet the cloth first and follow the manufacturer's instructions. To reduce the chances of seepage, it is safer to choose a dye which does not need soaking for a long period. Cold-water dyes will dye linen, cotton, silk and viscose rayon, and they are colourfast. As always with tie-dyeing, the cloth must be dried very thoroughly before untying to prevent any further leaking of the dye into the tied-off areas.

Tritik can be used to make straight lines, squares, curves, circles, zigzags and many combinations of these. It is a good idea to mark in the course the thread is to take with tailor's chalk. Use a ruler for straight lines and be sure you find the straight 'grain' of the fabric. Coins, tin lids or plates will produce circular patterns.

You can make a parallel line of motifs on the cloth by folding the fabric double and stitching through both layers, or make a full motif, such as a circle, by stitching an arc using the fold line as the diameter. Later, when the cloth is unstitched and opened, the full circle will appear. By combining different geometrical shapes a host of other motifs can be made.

When stitching you should always start a new thread at sharp angles so that it will be easier to gather, and you should normally stitch the entire pattern before you begin to gather. Stitches can be

*The different stitches shown on the left produce the patterns shown on the right when the cloth is steeped in a vat of green dye.*

criss-crossed and lines can be curved as well as straight, but in making the design, remember that you must be able to gather the cloth.

Machine stitching, especially where long straight lines are required, can be done on a sewing machine and makes the job that much quicker. Wind buttonhole or strong linen thread on the bobbin and use strong cotton or fine linen thread for the needles. Work a long, slightly loose stitch and do not attempt to do a very long length in one go. Stop every metre (yard), knot the ends of the thread, cut and begin again. To gather, pull the stronger bobbin thread very gently, making sure that there is a thick knot on the other end. When pulled tight, the end you are holding can be threaded through a crewel needle and a back stitch made, or you can bind the fabric and knot to finish.

## Special effects with tritik

An oversewing stitch over a fold makes a delicate 'fishbone' pattern for a border or as a central motif. Weights can also be used to produce original effects on cloth which has been gathered in circular patterns. The circle will produce a pucker when gathered, and after being dyed in a light or medium tone an extra spot of colour may be given to the tops of each pucker; this is done by hooking the centre point of each pucker onto a safety pin and then attaching the pin to a heavy object such as a metal nut (fig.3). The weighted centres can then be dipped in a darker dye or one of a different colour. This will produce cloth with a white pattern on the background colour which the material was first dyed, and there will be another tone in the centre of the circles.

Wooden dowels or rectangular shapes of wood can be used to obtain particularly delicate effects on fine materials by ruching the cloth over the wood. Be sure the wood is smooth, however, to prevent catches on the cloth. To do this fold the fabric along the 'straight' grain of the material (or from corner to corner of a square to get a diagonal fold) and stitch a line along the fold that is 6mm ($\frac{1}{4}$in) wider than the width of the dowel or wooden plank. This is to make a channel for the wood. Now insert the dowel or plank and gather the cloth as tightly as possible, using a knitting needle to ease the ruches. When the cloth is tightly packed, wind the thread two or three times round the gathered or ruched fabric and finish with a back stitch. You can also alternate round dowels and rectangular strips, but it is important to keep them at definite intervals, and make sure they stay parallel.

Dye the cloth with the ruching rod sticking up out of the bath if it is too long to be immersed.

3.

*On cloth which has been tied to give circular patterns, weights can be used to great effect. When the cloth has been dyed once, weights can be added to the circle centres which are then dipped in the dye once again to give them a darker colour.*

# Batik

# Introduction to batik

The word batik (pronounced bateek) means 'wax writing' and this is basically what batik is. It is a way of decorating cloth by covering part of it with a coat of wax and then dyeing. The waxed area keeps its original colour, and when the wax is removed the contrast between the dyed and undyed areas makes the pattern.

The exact origins of batik are unknown, but the technique was used in the Orient, long before printing was invented, to enhance the appearance of fine garments. Batik became most deeply rooted in Indonesia, particularly the island of Java, where it had become a highly developed art by the 13th century. Batik was considered a fitting occupation for aristocratic ladies whose delicately painted creations, based on bird and flower motifs, were a sign of cultivation and refinement, just as fine needlework was for European ladies of a similar position.

Java is still famous for batik, and the traditional patterns, developed over centuries, are still part of Javanese dress, although very few are made by the traditional method of wax painting. This, instead, has been rediscovered and put to use by craftsmen all over the world who find that the freedom of working with liquid wax, and the control of colour possible through dyeing, make batik an exciting and uniquely expressive medium. Increasingly, the all-over patterns of Oriental batiks are being replaced by imaginative pictures and designs of all sorts, which are used to make wall hangings and soft sculpture as well as decorations for clothing and household items.

Part of the attraction of batik is its simplicity, and the fact that you do not have to be artistic in the conventional sense to produce beautiful results. Some of the best effects in batik are in fact the work of chance. This is particularly true of the way in which the wax cracks to let small quantities of dye through, adding an unexpected and interesting effect to any design. This hairline detail, or 'crackling', is a special characteristic of most batik work.

Because batik wax is applied hot it is necessary to work fairly rapidly and this can produce a freedom (or loss of self-consciousness) that makes many people who think they cannot draw find, to their amazement, that they can. Of course, designs can be worked

*These brilliantly coloured batik fabrics from Sri Lanka (Ceylon) fully illustrate the impact of batik as a medium. Batik is a way of decorating cloth by painting designs on it in liquid wax. When the cloth is dyed, the waxed areas keep their original colour.*

out beforehand and for many things, such as borders and trimmings, this is necessary; but designs drawn spontaneously in wax, or according to the briefest sketch, can bring surprising rewards. Combined with the pleasure of drawing freehand is the fascination of working creatively with dyes – blending and mixing colours – to get as vivid or as subtle a shade as you want.

## Fabrics

Natural fabrics, such as cotton, linen and silk, are the most suitable. Viscose rayon can also be used, but avoid all synthetic fibres, no matter how closely they simulate natural fibres. Their true nature is revealed in the dyebath, by which time it is too late. They will not dye properly with cold dyes, which must necessarily be used for batik; otherwise the wax would melt in the dyebath. To test fibres of which you are uncertain, try this quick test. Watch carefully as you hold a single fibre over a lighted match. The synthetic thread melts quickly into a hard residue. Organic fibres burn more slowly, and a soft ash is formed.

Silk is one of the best fabrics for batik – the finer woven the better – and a finer waxed line can be drawn on silk than on any other fabric. However, silk is by no means indispensable, and the expense may inhibit your inventiveness since you will be less willing to take a chance. Cotton is excellent, and some prefer it to silk on the grounds that the sheen of silk obscures the pattern. In general, with coarser spun fabrics, more wax is absorbed and a fine sweeping line is harder to obtain, for the wax sinks rapidly into the cloth as it is applied. So, although you can batik canvas, calico and flannelette, these are only suitable for large, clear designs. For intricate work and, in particular, for pictures or wall hangings, fine linen or fine cotton is recommended. Especially delicate designs can be produced on batiste or cotton lawn – any thin cotton in fact which is not so transparent that your picture will look ghostly.

## Dye

Batik dye must be a cold dye since hot water would cause the hardened wax to melt in the dyebath. Ordinary cold-water dyes are best for beginners and all contain instructions for their use. However, after some experience you may prefer to use special, fast-acting cold dyes or vat dyes, which involve the use of additional chemicals but which 'take' a lot more quickly and, in the case of vat dyes, give exceptionally colourfast results. Once you are used to working with wax you can begin to experiment more with mixing dyes, buying the basic colours in bulk and making others yourself, as described earlier in the book.

---

### Beginner's equipment

**You will need:**
Some old white sheets. Old, torn white cotton sheets have the advantage of being already free from chemical finishes (which would otherwise prevent the dye from penetrating).
Note: all new fabrics must be boiled to remove the finish.
Candles (at least one containing beeswax).
Double boiler, for melting wax.
Good quality artist's paintbrush.
Cold-water dye and fixative.
Charcoal, or pencil, for making preliminary sketch.
Old picture frame. (Batik is normally worked on a special frame on which the cloth is tacked to keep it taut, but for beginners an old picture frame will serve just as well.)
You will also need to use the stove, or (more convenient) a hot plate or chafing dish (such as a fondue dish with candles beneath) to melt wax, and you will need access to a sink or a bowl for dyeing.

# Wax

The ideal mixture for batik work is 30% beeswax to 70% paraffin wax, and to try it for the first time you can easily melt down candles. If, however, you decide to do more batik, it makes sense to buy the wax in bulk from a craft supply house.

Beeswax adheres well to fabric, whereas paraffin wax is brittle, cracking easily. So the way in which you mix the two determines the amount of crackling that will take place. Crackling produces the fine lines that characterize most batik work. With pure paraffin wax there is the danger of it peeling off in the dyebath. A mixture of beeswax and paraffin wax therefore assures adherence, plus decorative crackling effects.

## How to batik

With a dark pencil or charcoal, begin to sketch your design on the cloth. It does not have to be elaborate – just a few guidelines. You can draw the first subject that comes to mind, or try the simple tree sketch in fig.1, which will give you some idea of the freedom of batik while providing a basic guideline at the same time. The tree motif illustrates another useful principle in batik – that it is often a good idea to work the surrounding spaces with wax rather than the object which is being depicted. So, in the case of the tree, it is the sky or the space around the tree that matters.

Fig.2 shows a simple geometric design which can be made using round household objects, like cups, to make the curves between the straight charcoal lines. You can add other shapes and innovations to this basic design as the illustrations show (figs.3, 4). Remember that you must decide whether you want the present colour of the cloth to be the background or the design itself, since this will determine where you apply the wax. When you have made your sketch, stretch the cloth across the frame and fasten it with tacks. You can prop the frame up with a book or block of wood to make the surface easier to work on.

To prepare wax, use either the stove or a hot plate. The latter is more useful since you can keep it beside you while you work. Otherwise, you will need to work beside the stove. When the wax is hot enough to use it will penetrate a test piece of cloth, sealing it on both sides so that light shines through easily and the fabric has a wet look. If the wax looks whitish and opaque, it has probably not penetrated. Place the wax beside you – to your right if you are right-handed, and to your left if left-handed – to avoid reaching over your work and possibly dripping wax on it unnecessarily.

You will need to work quickly as the wax cools and dries rapidly on the brush. Stir the wax frequently and let excess wax run off

*1a.*    *1b.*

*Simple freehand sketches are ideal for batik. In 1a., the tree itself is waxed and will show white on the finished product whereas in 1b. the surrounding area is filled in.*

before removing the brush from the pan. Fill in the design with wax, following your charcoal lines. Let the width of your brush determine the thickness of the line. Do not go over the same place twice – this has no effect – but paint on boldly, continually renewing the flow of wax on your brush. You can also make dots and lines by dripping wax directly onto the cloth from lighted candles, and this is often a good way to get your first sense of the wax technique since virtually no preparation is needed. If the shape you have made suggests any further shapes to you, then add them.

When your wax sketch is finished you are ready to begin dyeing. Unpin the cloth, crumple it a little to encourage the wax to vein and crack, and immerse the waxed cloth in the dyebath for the period of time recommended by the dye manufacturer. When you

*2, 3 and 4. By experimenting with basic geometric shapes you can develop design ideas for batik. Starting with three lines crossing at a point, and circles drawn round teacups, this simple design was elaborated into the motif shown opposite.*

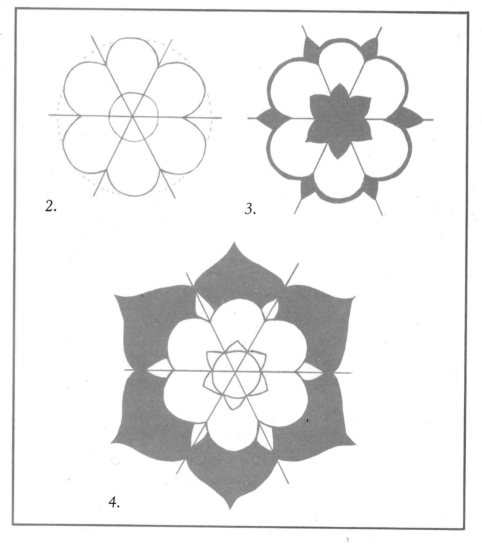

remove the cloth from the dyebath, hang it up to drip, preferably over a bowl or sink. Do not rinse, wring or dry by artificial means – impatience at this point is only rewarded by pale and uneven dyeing. Leave the cloth to drip-dry thoroughly. Remember that all dyes look several shades darker when wet, so don't worry if the fabric looks excessively dark at first.

If you want to enlarge on the design by adding more colour, do not remove the wax. Instead, when dry, pin it to the frame again and wax any new areas. Bear in mind that these areas will retain the colour of the first dyebath, and that in the unwaxed areas the colour of the second dye will blend with that of the first. If you are dyeing the cloth the same colour the second time, remember that you can only dye to a darker shade – light blue to navy, for example.

*Left: When the cloth has been stretched on a frame the motif can be painted on in wax.*

*Below: After the waxed cloth has been dyed blue, then it can be put back on the frame and the design can be enlarged.*

To remove the wax, iron it off between sheets of newspaper or boil it off in water. Wax can also be scraped off but this is not recommended for beginners since it is too easy to cut the cloth and ruin the whole thing. After scraping, boiling or ironing, a small residue of wax will still remain on the cloth, giving it a wet look which you may find desirable for wall hangings and other decorative devices, but for clothes and soft furnishings all traces of wax must be removed. This is best done by dry-cleaning or soaking the cloth in a strong detergent.

It is worth being rigidly neat about putting away dyestuffs and cleaning up after you have finished work. Use a sieve to empty the dyebath, since wax would accumulate in the drain.

*In the final stage the blue cloth is dyed red, producing purple on the areas free of wax. Once the cloth is dry the wax coating is removed with a hot iron.*

# Batik tools old and new

Several different methods of applying wax to cloth have developed over the centuries. The best one to use depends somewhat on the effect you want to achieve. Tjantings (pronounced jantings), the traditional batik tools, have brass cups which hold the wax. They have a thin spout through which the wax flows onto the cloth just as ink flows through a fountain pen. Tjantings can be bought in craft shops, and different sizes produce different widths of line. The tjanting is a drawing tool designed to make the delicate, fine lines which are the hallmark of traditional Javanese batiks, and the tool is still highly desirable for very fine work. An artist's brush has to be dipped several times into the wax to complete a long line or curve, thus interrupting the continuity and making the line unsteady, but the tjanting carries its own supply of melted wax which continues to flow through the spout as it is drawn across the cloth. The cup is refilled simply by dipping it into the hot wax.

To draw with a tjanting, fill the wax cup and stand the spout against something firm, to keep the wax from running out before you are ready to begin. Then trail the spout across the fabric where a line is desired. For very fine 'hairlines', draw the spout lightly and rapidly across the cloth. For broader, more definite lines press a little more firmly and move slowly across the surface. The tjanting may also be used successfully to produce swirls and dots. Practice is valuable because you must not only work rapidly but also learn to start and stop without making drips. When you want to stop, reverse the direction of the tjanting over the line you have just made, until you can get a lid beneath the tjanting to stop the flow of wax. The motifs can either be repeated, or used as part of a larger picture.

Tjaps are wax stamping tools and were also developed in Java. In the course of time many batik designs became well-established, each with its own name, and it became evident that these patterns could be more quickly applied to cloth by printing with wax. It made no sense to draw a repeated pattern over and over again – what was needed was a master image. Traditional Javanese tjaps are copper printing blocks (highly decorative objects in themselves)

*The flowing lines of this pattern were drawn with a tjanting – a traditional Javanese batik tool which gives a continuous flow of liquid wax.*

that print a design, or part of it, in the same way as a rubber stamp does, except that the tjap uses wax instead of ink. Tjaps not only make traditional batik designs less expensive, but they also open up a range of possibilities for craftsmen. Traditional Javanese tjaps are no longer exported, but improvised tjaps or stamping tools can still be very useful.

Improvised tjaps can be made from many familiar items around the house – corks, whisks, potato mashers and empty tin cans will all make a 'print' uniquely their own. They can be assembled by mounting any number of items on to a square of plywood or hardboard (fig.1) to make a relief surface.

To use a tjap, dip it in melted wax that has a depth of no more than about 12mm ($\frac{1}{2}$in). Shake excess wax back into the pan. Holding folded paper beneath the tjap, move it across to the right place on your cloth and stamp it down. Always re-wax the tjap between each stamp.

## Dyes

There are basically two kinds of dyes that are suitable for batik: cold-water dyes and vat dyes. Both are colourfast, and because they are strong you should always wear old clothes, an apron or an old shirt – rubber gloves are essential. Have your batik prepared before you mix the dyebath because the dyes lose their strength very quickly, and should be used at once. To prevent uneven dyeing, remember to wet the cloth thoroughly before immersing it in the dyebath for the specified length of time.

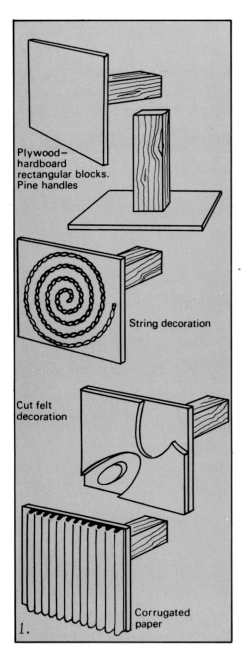

Plywood–
hardboard
rectangular blocks.
Pine handles

String decoration

Cut felt
decoration

1.

Corrugated
paper

*Tjaps can easily be improvised
by mounting any suitable printing
surface on a square piece of
of hardboard and fixing a
handle to the back.*

Although not as well known to craftsmen as cold-water dyes, vat dyes are the quickest and most colourfast of all. You can use them on cotton, silk, linen and viscose rayon. They give a range of brilliant colours, and their exceptional fastness is especially appealing for batik since the labour, and often the artistic merit, is deserving of long life. Vat dyes have the disadvantage that they require the use of two corrosive chemicals – caustic soda and a reducing agent, such as sodium hydrosulphite, which makes the dye temporarily water-soluble. (Some colours require salt.) The chemicals can be bought with the dye from craft shops which sell vat dyes, and at least one brand has the chemicals and dyes already mixed. Always prepare the dyebath according to the manufacturer's instructions.

Vat dyes develop through exposure to heat and light, and it is impossible to tell the colour until it is on the fabric. Neither the fine powder in the container nor the colour of the dyebath bear any resemblance to the developed colour. Vat colours take almost instantly, however, and you can quickly see the colour on the cloth. When you are mixing vat dyes to get a special shade, the problem caused by not being able to see the colours can be overcome by dipping a strip of fabric in the bath. The colour will appear at once on the fabric.

Cold-water dyes require the addition of washing soda and salt in the dyebath. The simplest of these dyes takes a long time to develop colour (normally one hour), and a quicker, though more complex, type is generally used for batik. Fast-acting cold-water dyes develop in between five and 20 minutes, depending on the intensity of the colour, and for best results should have the additional chemical compound, urea, added to the dyebath. This acts as a dye dissolver and guarantees a richer colour.

When you immerse wet cloth the colour change is immediate, but you should leave the fabric in the dye for at least five minutes to make sure of penetration. For dark shades it may be necessary to leave it for up to 20 minutes. For lasting colourfastness on work that will be washed frequently, or which you are anxious to preserve for as long as possible, the special additional fixing processes covered below are advisable.

When the dye has taken (whether you have used hot or cold water), remove the cloth and hang it on a clothes line. A plastic line and pegs are best as these can be wiped or washed after use to remove any left-over pigment. Make sure the cloth does not hang in folds but is spread out, as folds tend to hold the dye and dry darker than the rest of the material.

It is a good idea to keep a record of what you dye so that you will

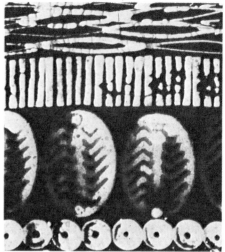

*Above: Results achieved with homemade tjaps. From top to bottom the materials used were: folded card, felt strips glued to wood, potato masher and felt stuck on a thread spool*

*Left: The intricately-made Javanese tjap in the foreground is typical of the large number of stamps which were used to print this tablecloth.*

be able to repeat any successful results and avoid disasters. Use a test strip. This means putting a narrow strip of cloth in each dye mixture and, as soon as it is dry, sticking it carefully into a notebook, making notes underneath, stating the number and quantity of dyestuff used.

## Removing wax

It is relatively easy to remove wax by ironing or boiling, but after some experience, and with considerable care, you will be able to remove most of the wax from cloth by scraping it off. The advantage of this method is that the wax can then be retrieved and used again. First cover a table with newspaper and lay the waxed fabric on top of it. Then, using a household paint-scraper or round-ended table knife which will be unlikely to pierce the cloth, scrape off as much of the hardened wax as possible. To remove the remaining traces of wax, place the cloth over a pad of newspaper, cover the cloth with another sheet of paper and iron it. The heat will cause the remaining wax to melt into the paper. Replace wax-coated sheets of paper with fresh ones until no further spots appear and all the wax has been removed.

## Fixing dye in cloth

Fixing takes place while the fabric is drying, after immersion in the dyebath. A warm, humid atmosphere accelerates the process, but cold-dyed batik lengths designed for use as dress or furnishing fabrics which need continued washing should undergo a further fixing process after the removal of the wax. Every designer has his preferred methods, so the techniques which may be employed vary considerably. Steam-baking, dry-baking, and air-drying are three which may easily be carried out at home and which need no additional or complicated equipment.

For all but the air-drying method, the finished fabric must be protected – wrapping it and lining it with paper towelling or old sheeting in such a way that the surfaces of the fabric do not come into contact with each other. The fabric must be lightly wrapped and folded.

If using the steam-baking method put the wrapped fabric on a shelf near the centre of the oven. Place a baking dish filled with water on the shelf below and bake at mark 7 or 220°C (425°F) for 15-30 minutes. Dry-baking involves also putting the fabric on a shelf near the centre of the oven, but not adding the tray of water. Bake at mark 7 or 220°C (425°F) for five minutes. Air-drying is even more straightforward. Allow the fabric to hang in a humid atmosphere for 48 hours. The bathroom is a good place if it is reasonably warm.

---

### Recipe for cold-water dye

There are several recipes for fast-acting cold-water dyes, but the one given here gives good colour, is easy to prepare, and can be used with any brand of this type of dye. The ingredients are usually all sold together.

Mix 1 teaspoonful of urea with 1½ jars of cold water (jars must hold ½ kilo or 1lb). Do this by adding urea to a whole jar of water, pouring this mixture into a plastic container or sink, then adding a ½ jar of cold water.

Now mix ½ – 4 teaspoonfuls of dye-stuff with two jars of cold water, and add to mixture in sink. (½ teaspoonful makes a pale shade, while 4 teaspoonsful is saturation point and makes the darkest possible shade.)

Mix ½ teaspoonful of soda ash and 1 teaspoonful of baking soda with ¼ jar of water and add to the rest. When you immerse wet cloth the colour change is immediate, but you should leave the fabric in the dye for at least 5 minutes to make sure of penetration. For dark shades it may be necessary to leave it for up to 20 minutes.

# Batik techniques

In nature there are no perfectly straight lines and no two things are ever exactly alike. Instead, there is an infinite variety of pattern and shape and it is this that makes batik appealing to the craftsman. Batik cannot produce the perfect regularity of design possible in assembly-line fabrics and it is wrong to try and use it to this end.

Whether you are building a picture or making a pattern, the basic design technique does not differ greatly. In both cases you will want to use all the space available in order to achieve an overall effect of balance and unity. You can do this by using basic design shapes, the most beautiful of which are often the simplest: circles, squares, and their variations – diamonds, checks, zigzags, stripes and spirals. The spiral is especially well-suited to batik. Embroidery and tapestry designs are also good sources of inspiration. Remember you are working with a liquid and therefore the more fluid shapes will produce the best results.

Crackling is the finely veined or 'marbled' effect so characteristic of batik. Originally it was considered a sign of inferior production, but it has come to be almost synonymous with batik – another case of the positive use of mishaps. For a crisp, delicate crackle the wax in the fabric must be very cold. The mixture of beeswax and paraffin wax must be just right. If the atmosphere is warm, the wax becomes pliable and crackling is unlikely to be successful. In warm weather the cloth can be put in the refrigerator for 10-15 minutes, or ice cubes can be added to the dyebath. In cold weather it is sufficient to hang the wax fabric out of doors. When the wax has become hard and cold, crease or crush the waxed areas. The direction of the cracks and the amount of crackling can, with practice, be controlled to suit the designer's intentions.

Do not attempt to imitate the regularity of other printing techniques. Instead work freely to exploit the possibilities of your design. The motifs in fig.1 show how different forms can be developed and explored. When you have developed your idea you can either make a small sketch to use for reference and enlarge and transfer it onto the cloth, or you can work by visualizing the finished work directly on the cloth. Finally you must decide which

1.

*Effective batik patterns can be developed by adapting and repeating basic shapes such as these flower motifs.*

45

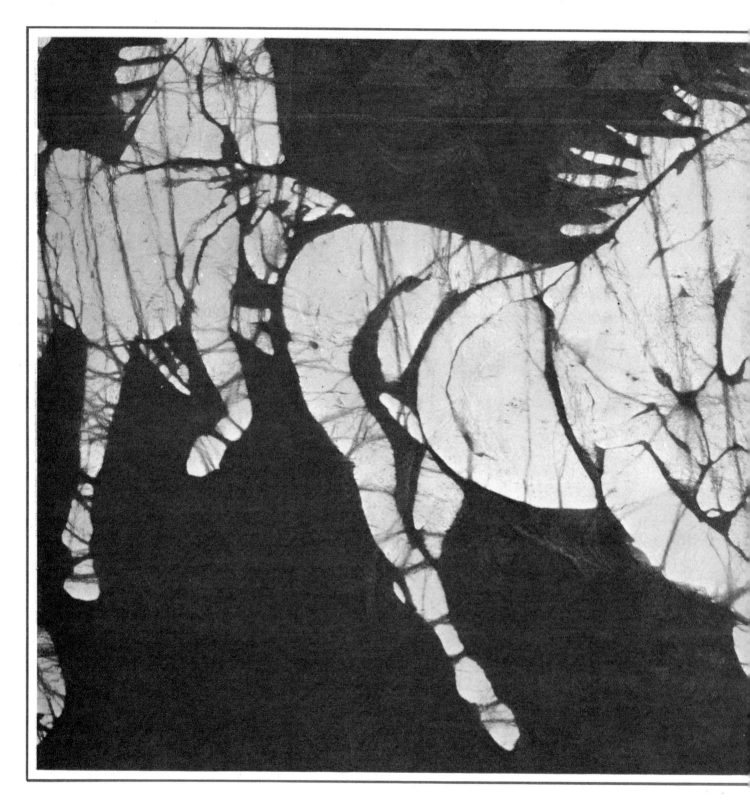

method of batik best lends itself to your chosen design. This will to some extend depend on your experience, but if there are fine lines, then the traditional tjanting may be useful, while one or more tjaps might be employed to accentuate or build up a design. Of the other methods that can be employed the most important is brush batik.

## Brush batik

Increasingly in modern batik work, craftsmen prefer to use a paint brush instead of working with a tjanting. Although it takes practice to use a brush effectively for fine work, a brush is easier to control, although it is often slower. For brush batik you will need a set of flat natural-bristle artist's brushes in several widths for filling in motifs and larger areas such as background, and a round, pointed oriental paint-brush for fine lines. Some craftsmen like a flat brush cut at an angle for making lines. These can be bought or you can cut your own by dipping the brush in wax and allowing it to harden before cutting the angle with scissors.

Wax tends to make brushes form 'whiskers' and these need constant trimming to keep their contour. Always dip your brushes in boiling water when you have finished. This will remove most of the wax and help preserve the life of your brushes. Batik brushes should only be used for batiking. Never leave them standing in wax as it will ruin their shape.

Wax temperature is very important in brush batik and the ideal temperature is about 120°C (253°F). Wax ignites at 170°C (338°F). If you are applying wax at the right temperature – a candlemaker's thermometer is a useful item – and at the right speed there will be no sign of brush strokes. However, it is always advisable to follow the general contours of the design with your brush.

You will find that it is only possible to apply wax over a small area at a time, especially in the beginning, and you may only be able to carry enough wax on your brush to cover a tiny area. But do not be impatient, the process will speed up as you go on and many batik patterns are made up of dots and discontinued lines, using this drawback to positive effect.

To use a brush, place it in the melted wax for a few seconds to allow it to become hot. Squeeze out surplus wax by pressing lightly against the side of the pan, then transfer the brush to your fabric, holding a piece of folded newspaper under the wax-loaded end to catch accidental drips. Apply wax to the cloth by pressing gently but firmly down onto the surface and pulling the brush along. As

*The crackling effect used here is made by crushing the cooled wax.*

the wax is worked into the fabric it develops a translucent appearance. Check constantly that the wax is penetrating through the cloth since both sides must be sealed to resist the dye. (If this is not achieved you may have to re-wax on the other side).

It is a worthwhile experiment to try making marks and lines with two or three different-sized brushes on an old sheet to get the feel of what each one can do best. Since wax hardens quickly you should always choose the size that will give you the quickest coverage with the most control.

To work successfully with a brush you must get into the habit of dipping it in wax very often and developing a rhythm until the motion becomes automatic. The wall hanging illustrated is a good example of brush batik. Made up of a tree, flowers and a human figure, it was inspired by a tarot card called Good Luck and Good Management – a remarkably fitting description of the necessary elements for working in batik.

## Reverse stencil batik

The great advantage of this method is that your otherwise unrepeatable pattern or outline can be to some degree reproduced. At least you are assured of getting the same size in any motif that is repeated. A reverse stencil is the part of a stencil that is normally cut away (fig.2). Reverse stencils can be made from contact paper, and the adhesive backing stuck onto the cloth. You then apply the wax round the paper outline. The stencil protects part of the surface from the wax just as wax protects the surface it covers from the dye. Take care not to use too much wax nor to allow the wax to become overheated, at too high a temperature, otherwise it may seep under the contact paper. Before dyeing, remove the reverse stencil. You can repeat the process after dyeing, shifting the stencil slightly to enhance the design.

## Over-batik

Over-batik not only produces very decorative effects, it can also mask mistakes or re-work designs that do not prove satisfactory. The method involves batiking a new design over an old one. It also solves certain problems of colour. For example, when you want to use a colour outside your chosen range (normally you would work from light to dark), one that would not blend or would upset the progression of shades, you can over-batik. To cover up mistakes, try over-batiking by brushing on wax in a series of whirls or spirals to link up and make a new, perhaps more decisive, pattern. Then dye it. Where you have over-batiked, your original pattern will be preserved, but within the context of the new design.

*A reverse stencil is made by using the part (on right) normally discarded.*

This brush batik picture was inspired by a tarot card and is made in four colours. The cloth was yellow to begin with, then it was dyed blue after the tree trunk and other yellow areas were waxed. Once more wax was added, for example in the sky and around the border, the cloth was dyed olive green. Then some areas of wax were scraped off and red dye was painted on. Finally all the wax was removed with a hot iron.

49

Above: Batik lends itself to picture making and with practice it is possible to achieve very impressive results.

Right: This attractive batik dress was made in Indonesia, the original home of batik.

# Painting on batik

Combining batik with conventional painting techniques adds another dimension to the art of batik. Wax is used as the resist in the traditional way but instead of being dipped the dye is painted on. This way colour is applied more precisely and a piece of work can be completed with only one waxing (although sometimes a second waxing gives greater depth and richness to a design). The wax resist enables you to paint the dye on the fabric without a thickener since the hardened wax keeps the dye from spreading beyond the required area.

## Materials and equipment

As with traditional batik, natural fibre fabrics, such as cotton and silk, are used. Silk and fine cotton are particularly suitable. Prepare cotton fabric as for batik, making sure that it is well ironed. Silk should simply be washed with mild soap flakes, then ironed. Materials and equipment are the same as for batik. Use fast-acting cold-water dyes. In addition, you will need a selection of soft brushes for painting, ranging from fine sable brushes for delicate work to decorators' brushes for large areas of colour.

## The method

When your fabric is clean, dry and ironed, stretch it on a frame. If you prefer, the fabric can be placed on several layers of newspaper and then attached to the paper with Scotch tape or masking tape. The paper must then be stuck to the working surface in the same way to stop it slipping about.

The design is applied to the fabric using a tjanting, or a brush, to draw the wax lines. Remember that an area to be painted in one colour must be completely surrounded by wax if you wish to prevent one colour running into another when the paint is applied. (Some designers occasionally let colours run together, to create special effects.)

Draw your design straight onto the fabric with the tjanting (or brush) if you feel confident, otherwise sketch it in first very lightly with a pencil. If you are using a transparent or semi-transparent

*The combination of batik and painting allows a great variety of colours to be used in close proximity, as on this shawl. Wax resist keeps the areas of colour separate until the paint has dried.*

fabric, the design can be drawn on a sheet of thin paper and placed under the fabric as a guide since the design will be visible through the fabric.

When you are satisfied with your waxed design, prepare the dyes and paint the fabric much as you would paint a watercolour. Alternatively, if you paint on one colour at a time, i.e. all the yellow areas and then all the green and so on, you will not have to rinse your brush quite so frequently.

When the dye has dried, a second coat of wax can be drawn, if desired, on some areas of the fabric not already waxed and finer detail can then be painted on. Allow the article to dry in a humid atmosphere for 48 hours. The dye will then be fixed. Remove the wax by ironing off between sheets of newspaper. The article should then be dry-cleaned to remove the last traces of wax.

*This silk scarf shows the kind of detail and colour that is possible with painted batik.*

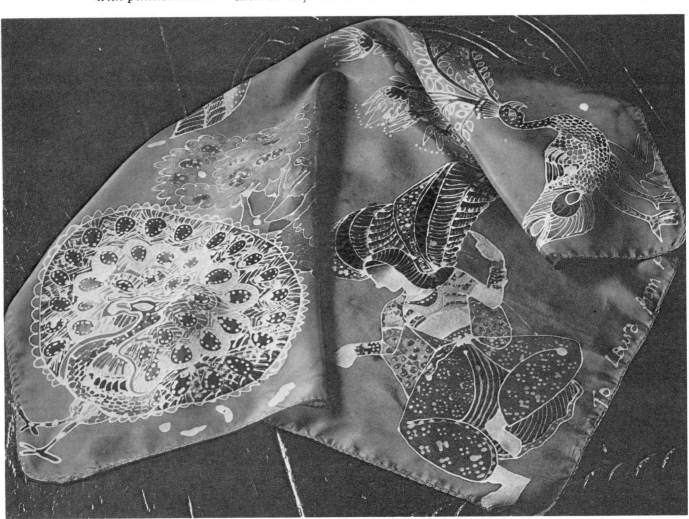

52

# Basic printing

# Relief printing techniques

To put it at its simplest, relief printing usually involves applying colour to one surface and pressing the colour onto another. You can print onto all sorts of surfaces including paper, cloth and walls: the type of paint or ink you choose will depend on what you are printing. Most relief and printing methods involve the making of a printing block, but there are many things which will print just as they are, needing no preparation. If the object, such as a leaf, is intricate and beautiful in itself, one single print may be best. If it is less interesting on its own then an endless variety of patterns can be made by repeating the printed impression. The arrangement of these impressions may be haphazard or ordered into lines, crossing lines or checks. The examples shown here have been printed with poster paint, printing watercolours, and oil-bound printing ink.

## Water-solvent paints
Poster paint has the disadvantage of drying up while you are printing and also tends to go into blobs, but this can add its own effective character to the print. It is best to use poster paint (or powder paint) diluted with very little water and applied with a stiff hog-hair brush. Printing watercolours do not dry so quickly and give a more faithful impression of the printing object. They may also be applied with a stiff brush, having first been diluted with a little water. To a certain extent, whatever you are printing will dictate the way in which the colour is applied. When printing with a hard, rigid object it is often best to spread the printing water-colour on a flat sponge with a knife. This then acts as a stamping pad. Poster paints should not be used in this way as they dry up.

## Oil-bound printing inks
To record the greatest amount of detail use oil-bound printing ink, which is best applied with a lino roller, available from most art shops. You will need a shiny, flat surface such as a piece of glass, mirror or plastic laminated board, on which to roll out the ink. When you are ready, squeeze some ink on the glass in a line as long as the width of your roller. Roll this out in different directions until

*Many types of fruit and vegetables are suitable for printing. Cutting a green pepper in half gives an ideal printing block which has been used here to print a glass mat. The seeds of the pepper were dabbed in with red dye on the end of matches.*

you have it evenly distributed. Don't spread it further than the area the roller covers in a single revolution as you will waste paint.

If you want to mix up a colour for printing, blend the inks together with a palette knife at the side of the glass and roll out the new colour. It is unsatisfactory to try to mix the colours by simply rolling them together. If you buy fabric-printing oil-bound inks you can use them on both paper and cloth. Printing watercolours may also be used on both materials.

## Preparing to print

Before you start printing, have some newsprint ready for test prints, the paper or cloth you plan to print on and rags for cleaning up and wiping your hands. If you are using oil-bound inks you will need some turpentine or white spirit for cleaning up as well. Be sure you have ample space in which to put the wet prints. You could rig up a temporary line with bulldog clips or clothes pegs

from which to hang the prints. Don't feel you must strive for a perfect impression every time; with this method of printing that is not possible and the mottled, irregular textures that result generate their own interest.

## Effects with different paints

Figs.1, 2 and 3 show the different qualities of each type of paint or ink. Fig.1 is a leaf printed with poster paint. Brush paint onto the back or more prominently veined side of the leaf. Lay the paper to be printed on a table with the painted leaf on top of it, paint-side down, and then place a piece of newspaper over the top. Press down carefully on the newspaper, making sure you cover all of the leaf. Pressure can also be applied with a clean roller. Then gently peel off the newspaper and the leaf from your print and hang it up to dry. In fig.2 the leaf is printed in the same way as fig.1 but with printing watercolour, therefore there is more definition than with

*Opposite: Familiar objects take on new guises when used as improvised printing blocks. The following articles were used to make the patterns shown here: screw head, broom closet clip, paper doily, wooden off-cut, thread spool*

1.

*Different types of paint produce different effects. In fig.1 a leaf was printed using poster paint, in fig.2 (overleaf) printing watercolour was used and in fig.3 oil-bound printing ink was rolled on.*

57

the poster paint. Fig.3 shows a leaf printed with oil-bound printing ink, applied with a roller. Detail is even clearer than with printing watercolour.

Once you have gained a little experience with the use of different paints you may wish to tackle something a little more ambitious. From printing patterns with leaves and other found objects it is a short step to making complete pictures. Figs. 4 and 5 show how a particular picture was made.

2.

*Above: A leaf printed with printing watercolour.*

*Right and far right: The working outline and the final result of a picture printed from a great variety of found objects. The blotchy effect was obtained by the choice of powder paint as a medium with which to work.*

# Printing with potatoes

Potato printing means, quite literally, using potatoes as printing blocks to stamp designs onto other surfaces. It is relatively inexpensive, depending of course on the price of potatoes, and allows you a wide variety of designs that can be reproduced on paper, fabric, wood or even plastic. Potatoes are an alternative to costly printing equipment and tools. Using only a kitchen knife you can cut motifs that can be stamped again and again. Moreover, designs do not have to be limited to the size of a potato since a larger design can be built up by repeating a single motif a number of times. Alternatively, a larger design can be made by using several different motifs together. Its low cost makes potato printing suitable both for beginners and for people who want to experiment with designs. If one block doesn't work it is easy and cheap to make another one. You simply wash, peel and cut a potato in half crosswise. Then cut in a sawing motion to get a flat surface. This is the surface that will be used to print.

## Cutting motifs

Motifs can be cut in several ways. So before you begin choose the one that best suits your design. A motif can be cut into the potato by making V-shaped cuts with a knife and gouging out the motif. Linoleum- or woodcutting tools can also be used. If you use this method the surface that will receive colour is the area surrounding the design – the design itself is recessed. The reverse of this method is also possible. By carving out the area surrounding the design, the motif you want to print will be left in relief to receive colour.

Most potatoes are roughly egg-shaped. When cut in half, an approximate circle is revealed which can be used to print similar rounded shapes like apples and plums, the sun and the centres of large flowers. But the technique that gives the greatest scope for printing with potatoes involves cutting the whole piece into a geometric shape as in fig.1. This way you get a number of forms – lines, squares, dots, triangles – that can be used repeatedly to produce a single larger shape or abstract design. By cutting the whole piece you also get a sharper printing edge and can see the rest of the

1.

*Above: Potatoes cut into geometric shapes for use as relief printing blocks.*

*Opposite: Potato printing gives a fresh simplicity to all sorts of surfaces as these colourful stationery ideas show.*

2.

*These designs are made from one potato block, printed in different directions. Top right: the block is repeated several times in the same position. Left: half the motifs are printed in as before and half are turned 90° to the left. Far right: the block has been printed at four different angles.*

design on the surface while you are printing. It is also easier to identify different blocks.

## About paint

Any paint that mixes with water is suitable for potato printing. The potato itself contains water and, for this reason, oil-bound paints or printing inks cannot be used. Watercolours, poster paints and tempera are all suitable for printing on paper and can be applied to the potato block with a brush or by using a piece of sponge as a stamping pad. To waterproof poster paint or watercolours on paper or card, spray with an artwork lacquer or fixative.

Acrylic polymer paint is excellent for most surfaces, being naturaally waterproof and hardwearing. It has to be applied with a brush as the paint dries too quickly to use the sponge method. Fabric paste dyes are very satisfactory for printing on cloth, but bear in mind that these are dyes, not paints, and by printing one colour over another you will produce a third, since they will blend automatically. This method can be used successfully with a little

3.

foresight. Cold-water dyes designed for use on natural fibres – cotton, wool, linen, silk – and on viscose rayon, should be used to get colourfast results. Apply the colour to the printing blocks with a paintbrush.

## To print

Cover the surface of your printing block with colour and press it down firmly but gently onto the surface you wish to print. If the motif is to be repeated, then recolour the block before you print again. This will guarantee an even colour throughout. Alternatively you can achieve variations in intensity by printing several times without recharging the block with colour.

As a general rule it is advisable to make a block for every colour you will need. Potatoes are fairly absorbent and the residue from the first colour may show through if another is used on top. If you are skilful however, you can use two separate colours side by side on one block. Always cut new blocks each day as potatoes tend to lose their firmness.

*As in fig.2, with this more elaborate, quarter-circle motif, a large variety of designs can be built up. The choice of colour can also be varied to useful effect.*

# Making a monoprint

Of all the traditional forms of print-making the monoprint (or monotype) is the simplest, easiest and cheapest. It requires very little in the way of equipment yet its sense of spontaneity and range of styles give it wide appeal. Monoprinting involves making an image or pattern on a flat surface such as glass, usually with printing inks, and then pressing paper or cloth against it to print the image. But unlike other forms of printing, it is only possible to make one print from the master image. William Blake used monoprinting in combination with etching, and Dégas, Toulouse Lautrec, Gauguin and Matisse have all explored its possibilities. Yet it is equally popular with young children because it is easy to do and invites complete freedom of expression.

## Materials

There are no strict rules about what you do and do not need in monoprinting, and the more you improvise the better. The main thing is to find the best way to achieve the effect you want, and basically to do this you will need colour, a printing surface on which to make the image, and some paper or cloth on which to print it. You should also bear in mind that your finished print will be a mirror-image of the design on the printing surface and in some cases this may make a difference.

Normally a sheet of glass is used as a printing surface, but any smooth, flat surface such as Formica is suitable. If the printing surface is somewhat larger than the material to be printed you can use one end as a palette for mixing inks. Oil- or water-based printing inks, available from artists' suppliers, are the best colours to use for paper (with oil-based inks you will also need some turpentine for diluting colour). For printing onto textiles use special fabric printing inks or dyes.

Paper is the traditional monoprinting surface and any fairly absorbent paper may be used, from the cheaper cartridge papers to the good quality, mould-made, hand-made and Japanese papers. Working with textiles can be more difficult than with paper, and beginners are advised to become used to the technique of printing

*Monoprinting is suitable for use on either paper or fabric and has a wide variety of applications. A number of different designs are combined in this attractive patchwork cushion.*

*Examples of monoprints from an artist's portfolio. Monoprinting is one of the most flexible and at the same time one of the simplest of mediums, and is ideal for use by children under a watchful eye.*

on paper first. When you are ready to print on textiles you can either use a fairly thin cloth such as calico or a heavier canvas of the type used in bookbinding. Always use a natural fibre (cotton, linen, silk) or viscose rayon, and cold-water fabric dyes.

The tools used for applying colour and making images depend entirely on your own imagination and on the type of image you want to produce. If the picture is to be multi-coloured you can apply ink to the printing surface with a paint brush just as you would apply colour to canvas, or you can use a palette knife (also for mixing inks). A roller for rolling ink onto the printing surface is invaluable and a small 10cm (4in) wide artists' roller should be sufficient. Large heavy printer's rollers are excellent but also expensive. Pencils, combs, or knitting needles can all be used

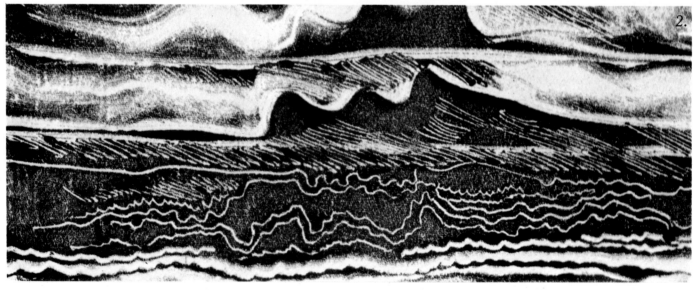

1.

2.

successfully to scratch images into the rolled out inks and if you use your fingers, sponges or paper towels you will get effective blotted effects and other textures.

## The method

Apply ink or fabric dye to the printing surface either by rolling it on with a roller or using a paintbrush, palette knife or other tool. Then when the design is ready, lay paper or cloth gently on top of the inked surface and rub the back of it carefully by hand. Print-makers often use the back of their closed fingers to do this; inky hands are unavoidable. You can lift one corner of the sheet very carefully to see how the paper or cloth is taking the ink. More rubbing may be necessary. Lift the paper off when the image has

*Different monoprinting techniques produce a fascinating variety of styles. 1. is made by painting on glass and pressing printing paper onto it; 2. uses incised lines; 3. involves splashing the printing surface; 4. drawing on the back of the print with a pencil.*

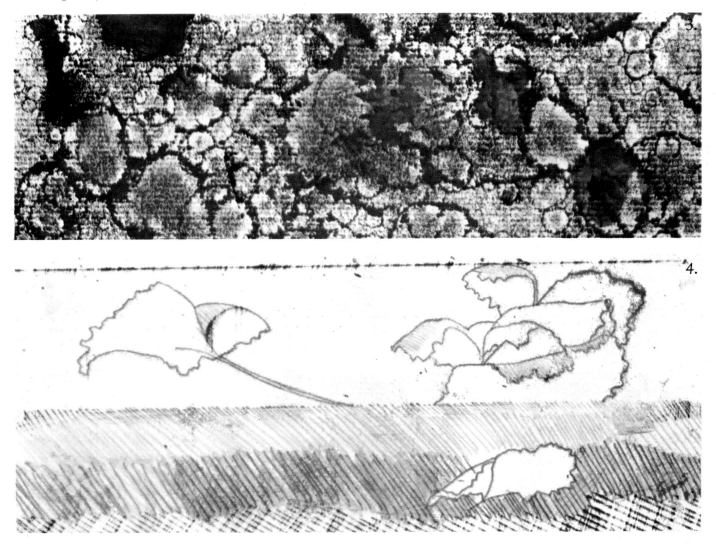

*Top: To make a monoprint, roll out colour onto a glass slab. The design is drawn with a matchstick and then the paper is lowered onto the glass.*
*Above: As the paper is lifted it reveals the image transferred onto it from the glass.*

been transferred onto it; this is the monoprint. Turn the print face up on a table top, or fasten it to a clothesline to dry. You can make further use of the residual ink on the glass or Formica and develop it into another image by reshaping or adding more ink.

## Monoprint techniques

Painting directly onto the glass with a paint brush, palette knife, fingers or anything that will make texture is a way of making a multi-coloured design or of painting a picture as you would on canvas (fig.1). If you want to paint an image but are uncertain of your ability to draw free-hand, you can make a preliminary pencil sketch and then slip it underneath the glass printing-surface. It will be visible through the glass and you can ink in the glass accordingly. Ink can be applied thickly, in the style known as impasto, or it can be thinned (if oil-based use turpentine, if water-based use water,) to create watercolour-type washes.

Incised drawing is a very easy way to work. Using a roller, cover the printing surface with an even film of ink (or, if you want a multi-coloured background, use a paint brush). The design can be drawn in with a pointed tool. Very little pressure is needed to slide the point over the glass and a free-flowing line can be made fairly simply. The point removes a small trough of ink from the glass, resulting in a white line on the finished monoprint (fig.2).

A variety of abstract images can be created by spreading oil-based ink freely and arbitrarily over the printing surface and then splashing it with turpentine or white spirit (fig.3). Introducing an element of chance, even in a carefully drawn design, often produces the most rewarding results. Happy accident is almost the essence of monoprinting, and designs where the fall of the paper and the spread and absorption of the ink have not been completely controlled are some of the most successful.

Delicate and exciting interpretations of line drawings can be made by the simple method of transfer drawing. Place paper or cloth over the inked printing surface and then draw with a pencil or ball-point pen on the back of the material while it is gently resting on the thin coat of ink. Do not apply pressure to any other area, the ink will prevent the print from sliding. Fig.4 shows a print made in this way. Similarly, you can press a leaf or other familiar object against the back of the material and this will print on the other side. The same film of ink if smoothed over will probably be enough for several monoprints made in this way.

Experimenting with different tools and consistencies of ink is part of the enjoyment of monoprinting. Different techniques can often be combined and new ones evolved from initial mistakes.

# Stencils

# Designing with bought stencils

Stencils are one of the easiest ways to paint pictures or do lettering on surfaces. Even if you can't draw you can be sure of getting a clear, professional-looking image, and the decorating possibilities are enormous. Usually a sheet of brown coated paper with a cut-out design, a stencil can be seen as a negative image since the shape you wish to paint has already been cut out, leaving a crisp outline. By putting the stencil against the surface on which you want to paint the image, you automatically mask out the area which should not receive paint and leave free the area which should. It is by painting this area, making sure your brush covers the entire free surface, that the image is printed. When the stencil is lifted your picture or lettering will be neatly visible on the object or paper beneath.

*Even the simplest stencils can give character and individuality to an otherwise commonplace object such as an eggcup.*

## Materials

Precut stencils can be bought in toy shops and from artists' suppliers. In range, these stencils may be somewhat limited but with a little ingenuity they can be combined and adapted to produce attractive, colourful results.

To begin stencilling you will need, as well as the stencils you have chosen, the right kind of paint for your surface. Another essential is masking tape with a low-tack adhesive. It can be used to fix the stencil in position and it will not mark the surface on which you are painting when it is peeled off. You should also have at least two stencilling or stippling brushes, one for light and one for dark colours. Sometimes a piece of plastic sponge can be used instead. Stencil kits, complete with stencils, brushes and watercolours are easily obtainable.

## About paint

Water-based paints, including artists' watercolours, acrylic polymer paint and poster paint can all be used for stencilling, but these should be used as dry as possible. After loading the brush with paint, blot it on a rag to remove excess liquid.

Acrylic polymer paints work extremely well if used undiluted and have the advantage of becoming waterproof on drying. In many cases, especially on hard surfaces, they are best applied with a small piece of close-textured plastic sponge. This material is very cheap and a new piece may be broken off for each colour.

Poster paint, again undiluted, may be used in the same way. If it is used on wood the application of several coats of polyurethane clear varnish, after the paint is quite dry, will render it waterproof and hardwearing as well as increasing the brilliance of the colours. Artists' watercolours are really only suitable for use on paper, while artists' oil paints are not found to be very satisfactory either. On wood a halo of slightly tinted oil tends to seep out around the edges of the design.

*Painting in the design is a quick and simple process once the stencil has been taped down.*

Enamels are not very effective when stencilled with a sponge or brush. They are rather liquid and must therefore be applied very sparingly. By this method one cannot achieve the depth and brilliance of colour normally associated with enamels. The exception, however, is the type of enamel paint available in an aerosol spray can. Follow the instructions on the can, using several light coats rather than one thick one. Each application dries in a few minutes. This type of paint may be used with success on non-absorbent surfaces such as glass and plastic. It becomes hard after about a week. When using spray paint the stencil must be firmly taped against the surface as the fine spray can penetrate even the tiniest gaps. Sometimes, of course, this shadowy effect, where the spray has crept under the stencil, can add a certain charm.

Sari relief colours, originally intended for the raised decoration on Indian saris, may be successfully stencilled onto glass and pottery. These should be used straight from the tube or diluted with a trace of copal varnish. Being oil-bound, they take a fairly long time to dry on a surface which is non-absorbent, especially if the atmosphere is damp. The manufacturers advise natural drying (and patience) as heating may cause the paint to craze.

## Masking tape

Masking tape serves a double function. It is used to hold the stencil in place on the surface and it also covers those parts of the stencil pattern which you do not wish to print. Multi-coloured designs are achieved by blocking out all areas that do not take the particular colour you are applying at the time. Later you mask the areas where you have applied the first colour and unmask the parts to receive the next. The flower pattern on the school fair poster uses the design with the flower in red and the stalk and leaves in blue. While stencilling the red, the blue parts were masked out and vice versa. By applying double-sided adhesive tape to the reverse side of a stencil, the outline can be more securely taped down. This is especially useful when using a spray paint or when applying a design to a curved surface, such as a glass, since the centre parts of the stencil otherwise tend to stand away from the surface.

## Lettering

When stencilling lettering, draw a pencil line on which the letters can rest. In the case of a material like glass, as with the glass storage jar, attach a strip of masking tape to mark this line. It can be removed later. Rule horizontal lines on the stencil from the base of the letters to the outside edges. When positioning the letters, match the lines on the stencil to those on the paper. This will help you to get the letters straight. Fig.1 shows how this is done. The spacing between the letters must be done by eye. If in doubt, you can lightly pencil the letter through the stencil before committing yourself to paint. Borders may also be lined up in this way.

When stencilling letters from a stencil sheet, temporarily block out the letters either side of the one you are actually printing as this avoids unwanted marks. Use masking tape or small pieces of paper held over the letters. To print tiny motifs, such as the flower on the egg cup and the napkin ring, it may be necessary to cut out that part of the stencil from the main sheet to make it easier to handle and stick down to the object being stencilled.

## Cleaning up

To clean a stencil wipe it gently with a rag, dampened with the solvent appropriate to the type of paint you are using. In some cases, as with the spray-on enamel or acrylic polymer paint, the stencil need not be cleaned. The thin layer of paint in fact strengthens the stencil and the paint will not stain the other paints that may be used later.

*Stencils can easily be applied to china or glass. Here they are used to label food storage jars.*

# Home-made stencils

*By cutting your own stencils you can produce designs tailor-made to your own requirements. These birds stencilled on the end of a child's cot echo the pattern on the blanket.*

The North American colonists were among the first to exploit the marvelous ways stencils can be used in home decoration. In 18th-century America, wallpaper was a luxury only the very wealthy could afford, but the colonists soon found that with a little imagination and patience they could simulate the elegance of imported, handblocked paper by cutting out designs in stencils. Using stencils they found that by repeating the same motif again and again the could achieve a uniform overall pattern just as good as one produced by fine printing techniques. For their designs the colonists turned to the natural world around them – willows, oak leaves, fruits – and to patriotic motifs like the American eagle. They did not stop at walls but stencilled floors to resemble floor coverings and other artefacts to look like items difficult to obtain in the New World. The result was a fresh, original style which is still popular. Just as the colonists adapted European styles to suit their needs and environment, their designs in turn can be adapted to modern tastes.

## General rules

When a surface is being stencilled it is important that it is properly cleaned or the paint will not adhere. Wax must be removed from floors and furniture and sometimes an old surface, such as a wall or trunk, must be repainted. If you are stencilling on an old, solid-coloured wall surface, scrub it before you begin.

The sort of paint you use will depend on the surface on which you are working. Many experts recommend poster colours, which can be sealed when dry with clear lacquer, but high-gloss surfaces such as mirrors or tiles should be stencilled with spray-on enamel. There is no reason why modern oil, emulsion or vinyl paints should not be used on walls. Acrylic polymer paint is hard-wearing and recommended for floors. Gold and silver paints can look most effective too. If you are using a mixed paint, be sure that you have prepared enough for the entire surface. It is difficult to mix and match a colour in the middle of a job, since a paint that is dry is never the same shade as when it is wet. Stencilling a wall can take a long time

To make up for the lack of patterned fabric and paper the American colonists made wide use of home-made stencils.

and mixed paint can be stored in a tightly closed container between sessions. Finally, when choosing your colourscheme, remember that it is difficult to stencil a light colour over a dark one as several coats may be required.

## Making a stencil

To make your own stencil first trace the outline of the pattern you

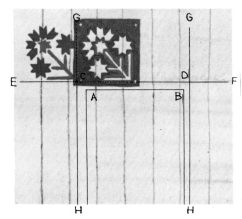

*Right: The stencilled motifs on this trunk were enlarged from the pattern of the lining paper.*

76

wish to use onto a sheet of paper. Any non-absorbent paper will do, but the most durable is oiled paper, available from craft shops. Place the paper on an old sheet of cardboard to avoid damaging your work-surface, and cut along the lines with a Stanley knife.

## Decorating ideas

Once you know how to make a stencil, the possibilities of stencil design are infinite. Ideas can come from many sources: the repetition or adaptation of earlier designs is one, while designs can also be traced from natural objects like leaves or based on existing motifs, as are the blue birds on the child's crib in the photograph, which have been taken from the quilt fabric. The positioning of the stencils also allows great scope for inventiveness. Tin and glassware, such as bread bins [boxes] and canisters, can be decorated or lettered with stencils, and suitcases, which all look so much alike, can be made identifiable by stencilling on initials, monograms or other personal motifs.

*This trellis design is used to give interest and colour to a low-ceilinged room in a country cottage. The design is printed in two parts, which are keyed in by holes punched in the corners of the stencil sheets.*

# Stencilling on cloth

*Materials for stencilling on cloth are not expensive: all you need are special flat-headed brushes, paste fabric dye, stencils and cloth to print on.*

Stencilling on cloth gives anyone with an eye for colour and an urge for creativity, wide-ranging opportunities for making changes in their home or wardrobe. A single stencilled motif such as a sailing ship or a palm tree, for example, is easy to cut out and can be stencilled onto a T-shirt or a table mat, the pocket of a blouse or the front of a laundry bag. Alternatively, stencilled motifs can be repeated over and over again to make a border or an all-over design. Delicate flower borders on sheets and pillow-cases or on the hem of a child's dress can be very effective, while all-over patterns can be used on a number of items, such as tablecloths, scarfs and shirts. Straw hats and baskets, satin shoes and canvas awnings can all be stencilled, and more ambitious designers can even stencil lengths of cloth. Beginners however, may prefer to stencil ribbons and tapes for trimming clothing or household items, since mistakes are not so disastrous as when made on the object itself.

## Materials you will need

Apart from the stencils themselves, you will also need masking tape, an old blanket or other padding material, newspaper, drawing pins or tacks and dressmaking pins. It is advisable to have two stencil brushes if you are painting with more than one colour – one for light and one for dark shades. These are obtainable at art shops. Although cloth can be stencilled with fabric paint, the best medium to work with is fabric dye in paste form. Liquid dyes tend to be too runny and fabric paint leaves a stiffness on the areas of cloth to which it is applied. Another advantage of dye is that it can be mixed, so only the basic colours need be bought. Fabric paste dyes are colourfast and can be used on natural fibres such as cotton, silk, wool or linen and viscose rayon. If you are not sure of the fibre content of the item you wish to stencil, test a sample with the eye to find out if it 'takes'. Remember also that dyes blend, so if you are stencilling blue onto yellow, the end result will be green.

In addition to coloured dyes you can also buy 'medium' to make colours lighter and more transparent. Medium is the colourless substance in which the dyes are suspended. When mixing medium with dye colours, always add the dye gradually to the medium until you reach the right shade. Acrylic polymer paint, which is waterproof, is the most suitable colouring for woven straw.

## Preparation

Before you start, make sure the fabric is free of creases. Iron it, dampening if necessary. If the cloth contains starch or dressing, you should wash it thoroughly before printing. Secure the blanket

*The red fruit stencils shown opposite look well printed in a grid pattern on cotton cushions.*

or padding material to the table-top, stretching it taut. This can be done by wrapping it round the table ends and taping it to the underside or fastening it with drawing pins or tacks. Put several sheets of newspaper on top of the secured blanket to soak up any excess dye that may go through. If the fabric you are stencilling is very fine, put some blotting paper on top of the newspaper for added absorption. Stretch out the fabric you intend to print and attach it to the blanket with pins.

If you are stencilling something double-sided like a pillow-case or shirt, slip some paper inside to prevent the dye from going through and marking the other side. If your design involves a repeated pattern, it is wise to pencil guide-lines very faintly on the cloth. Small holes in the corners of the stencil paper can be useful for this purpose. For dark fabric use tailor's chalk which can be brushed off without any difficulty.

## To stencil

Fasten the stencil to the fabric with pieces of masking tape and put some of the dye into a shallow container. Do not overload the brush with paint but take enough to allow you to work with ease and in control of the brush. Using white dye or a very light colour mixture may make it necessary to stencil the image twice. If so, let the first coat dry before applying the second and line the stencil up carefully using punched holes in the stencil paper corners. With multi-coloured designs, stencil the first colour and let this dry before proceeding with further colours. When the finished item is thoroughly dry, iron it from the back, according to the dye-manufacturer's instructions, to fix the dye. When washing later on, use care and do not wring.

## Reverse stencilling

With reverse stencilling a mask or template of the shape of the design is used to prevent the paint from reaching the surface to be decorated, so that the design is painted round the outside of the shape. This technique can be used on any sort of surface from walls to fabric. Use double-sided tape to fix the template to the surface. Then, if the colour is to reach right to the edge of the surface, apply colour in the usual way. Alternatively the area of colour can be contained by making a larger, square mask to frame the colour. You can also fade out the colour gradually by stippling, i.e. by varying the pressure of the brush when you apply dye or paint. For walls or furniture, aerosol spray paint is also effective. Use the cut-out part of any ordinary stencil to build up an alternating 'positive/negative' design.

*The lamb is a reverse stencil made using a template from a child's drawing set.*

# Linocuts

# Making a linocut

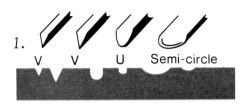

*Linocutting tools are normally V- and U-shaped. The top diagram shows the grooves different cutters make, while the lower diagram shows how and how not to make a groove. Do not make your grooves too steep-sided or the printing surface will be undermined.*

'Lino' printing is derived from wood cuts, one of the oldest forms of painting, and works in much the same way. You make your design by carving away unwanted parts of a block – in this case linoleum – then you cover the surface of the block with ink and press paper against it to print the design. The sections that have been gouged out are not inked and print white (or the colour of the paper). The contrast makes the printed design. Linoleum is, of course, much easier to cut than wood and is cheaper as well.

## Equipment

The equipment needed for lino cutting is simpler than that for other traditional forms of printing and all materials can be bought from art and craft suppliers. Kits are also on the market containing all the basic tools and materials.

Lino cutters are gouging tools specially designed for engraving linoleum blocks. They are shaped to make U and V cuts and come in several sizes. To begin, you should have a small and a medium sized V-shaped cutter and a small and a fairly large U-shaped one. Tools can be bought either with individual handles or with interchangeable cutters which fit into the same handle.

To sharpen tools you should use an oilstone and rub it gently against the outside edges so as not to bend the blade. Inside edges can be sharpened with a slip, as very narrow oilstones are called. Triangular slips are available for V shapes.

A craft knife such as a Stanley knife, lino-cutting knife or mat knife is essential for cutting linoleum blocks to size. A printing roller or crayon and a slab to roll out inks on are also needed, and small, cheap rollers are available for this purpose. The slab can be a sheet of glass, Formica, hardboard or Masonite.

Cartridge paper is suitable for linocut printing and there are many different Japanese tissues made especially for block printing but these are more expensive. It is worth experimenting with all sorts of papers but avoid very shiny paper since this is non-absorbent and does not take ink well.

Linoleum should be the old-fashioned, canvas-backed matt-finished type, not the vinyl flooring which is commonly used today. Genuine linoleum suitable for lino cutting can be bought from art suppliers, usually in several different sizes ranging from a small square the size of your hand up to a square metre (yard) or so. The larger pieces can be cut as required with a craft knife.

Use oil-based printing inks cleaned up with turpentine or white spirit or printing watercolours, cleaned up with water. Both inks are available in a good range of colours. For mixing inks you will need a palette knife or old table knife and some rags for cleaning up. To make a good print you will require pressure and this can be achieved by either burnishing or rubbing the back of the paper with the back of a tablespoon handle or the bottom of a glass.

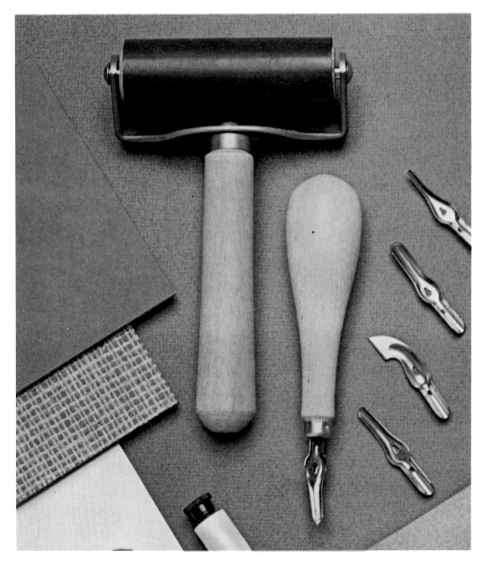

*Linocuts are made by gouging out parts of a linoleum square, inking the surface and printing it. The materials needed are shown on the left: canvas-backed linoleum sheet, roller and slab, linocutting tool with interchangeable blades, ink and paper.*

83

Alternatively, you can use a small screw-down printing press or, for small prints, a flower press.

## How to cut a lino block

Before you begin to cut your first design, experiment a bit in order to find out what sort of cuts your tools will make. See how many different lines and textures you can make and remember that the purpose of your tools is to gouge out the parts of the block that you do not want to receive ink. It is by recessing these areas that the ink is prevented from reaching them when rolled onto the surface of the linoleum block.

To cut: hold the ball of the handle against your palm and guide the tool with your thumb and forefinger, with the V or U turned up. Push the tool gently forward to make a groove. By turning the block as you go you will be able to make a curved line. U-shaped gouges give a wider line and can also be used to create a pebbled effect. Broad U or semi-circular gouges are for removing large areas. The angle of the cuts should slant upwards as shown in fig.2 so

*Top: The peacock design must first be traced on a linoleum block of the same size.*
*Above: The design is made by gouging out areas of the block with cutting tools.*

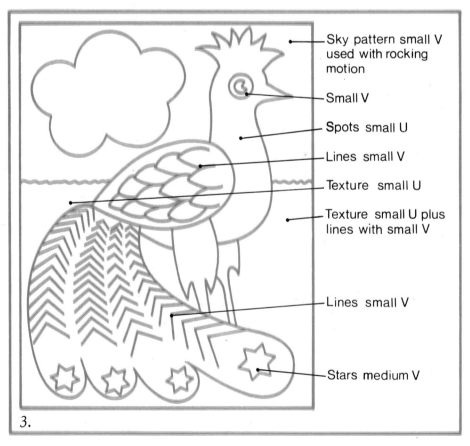

Sky pattern small V used with rocking motion

Small V

Spots  small U

Lines  small V

Texture  small U

Texture  small U plus lines with small V

Lines  small V

Stars  medium V

3.

To print, ink must first be rolled out evenly on a slab.

The ink is then rolled from the slab onto the lino block.

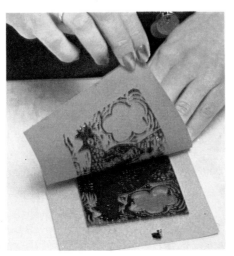

Far left: Paper is lowered onto the block and then burnished.

Left: When the paper is peeled off the finished print appears.

that the printing surface of the block remains firm. To avoid cutting your fingers in case the tools should slip, keep the hand holding the linoleum block firmly behind the cutting hand as much as possible. Begin with the peacock motif shown and cut a piece of linoleum the same size as your design, in this case 8cm by 10cm ($3\frac{1}{8}$in by 4in). It is easiest to cut through the hessian backing with a knife and then crack the linoleum apart. Trace the pattern (fig.3) onto the lino block and, using the gouges indicated in the diagram, cut away unwanted parts of the block as indicated with the small U- and small and medium V-shaped gouges. When you have finished cutting your block always make sure there are no loose bits of linoleum left on the block since these will stick to the roller, mess up the ink and spoil your print.

## How to print

Before you begin to ink your block, make sure you have plenty of table space, including an area on which your wet prints can be laid out to dry. Spread newspaper or old cloth over the working surface. Once you have inked the printing block you will have to print immediately, so cut the paper to size first, allowing a generous margin all around.

Squeeze a line of ink the length of your roller onto the inking slab. Now roll this out, rolling in several directions to make sure the ink is distributed evenly. Roll ink from the slab onto the surface of your linoleum block, again rolling in different directions and recharging the roller with ink as necessary.

To print by rubbing, place a piece of printing paper on the inked block and gently but firmly rub with a spoon handle or other similar tool, working from the centre outwards. If you are printing on delicate paper do not rub the print directly as it may tear. Place a thin sheet of white paper on top and then rub. Do not rip the printed paper straight off the block. Lift a corner carefully to see if more rubbing is needed. The paper will flop back into place again.

To print in a screw-down press you will need two pieces of stiff cardboard to fit inside. Put a flat pad of newspaper on top of one sheet of the cardboard, then put your printing paper on this and put the inked surface of the lino block face down on the printing paper. Cover this with the other sheet of cardboard and put the whole sandwich into the press. It is only necessary to nip or press it for a moment; there is no need to leave it sitting in the press.

After taking one print, simply re-ink the block and print again. You don't have to clean the block between prints. Proceed to make as many copies as you wish; and when you have finished clean up all equipment and the block itself with the appropriate solvent.

*Opposite: Peacock note cards can be printed in a variety of colours by using different coloured papers and printing inks. Alternatively a limited edition of prints can be made on white paper.*

# Printing cloth with linocuts

*When linoleum printing with fabric dyes, it is necessary to coat or 'flock' the surface of the linocut with powdered fibres so that it will become absorbent and hold the dye.*

Linocut designs can be successfully printed on cloth as well as on the paper surfaces already described. The linocut is derived from the earliest form of printing on cloth – the wood block – and the printing method is virtually the same for both. Likewise the applications are very similar. Linocuts can be used to print curtain material and other furnishing fabrics, table mats, wall hangings and dress fabric. The main advantages of linoleum as a medium are that it is cheaper, and more easily available than specially cut wood, and is also quicker to work.

## Designing for fabric printing

This is a fascinating occupation in itself and its practical applications can be even more rewarding—you can transform the linen cupboard, the clothes you already have or those you intend to make. On clothing, a single motif printed on a patch-pocket or a handkerchief can be attractive but you can take better advantage of the printing medium by stamping your design repeatedly along the hem of a skirt or all over some napkins. Household linens make excellent printing surfaces, but remember you will be working with colours that 'take' on natural fibres, and not on mixed fibres or other synthetics. Suede, another natural fibre, can also be decorated with linoleum designs and a tan suede coat, for example, with a dark brown motif printed on a pocket or a delicate border decorating the edges would look very original.

To best exploit the potential of lino decoration on clothing, however, it is advisable to print the cloth before the garment is made up. Either print a length of cloth in an all-over pattern of your own design or cut out the cloth and then print motifs that follow or complement the contours of the garment. By following the shape of the cut-out pattern you can decorate the curve of a shoulder line or a neckline and by printing a garment before it is sewn you can position motifs more accurately. To position motifs on garments it is wise to print the motif (or motifs) on paper first and cut it out. Then you can arrange it exactly where you want it to go and either mark or outline the position with tailor's chalk.

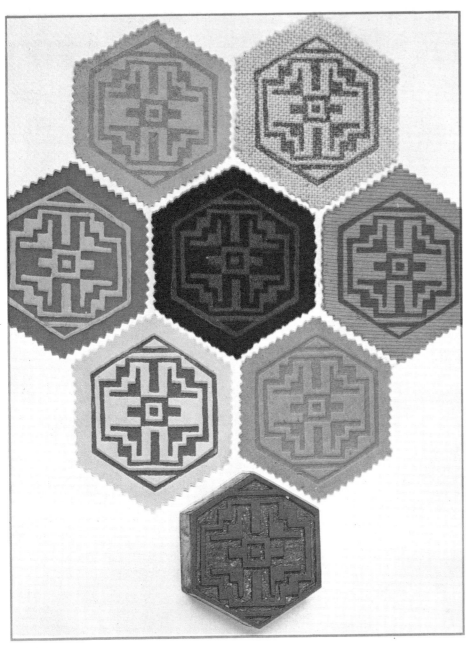

*Linocuts can be used to print a wide variety of fabrics. Here the same block has been printed on (reading from top left to bottom right) suede, hessian, rayon, velvet, cord, silk and cotton.*

## Colours

Fabric can be printed using either fabric-printing inks or cold-water fabric dye in paste form. Both work equally well but the methods of printing are slightly different so choice depends largely on personal preferences and availability. Fabric-printing inks do tend to give a slight stiffness to cloth but this can be quite effective. Both ink and fabric paste dyes are widely available.

## Printing with inks

There are two ways to use fabric-printing inks; the first, a straightforward stamping technique, is very similar to printing on paper while the second involves mounting the lino block on wood and hitting it with a mallet to print. This method is easier to use if the motif is to be repeated. Block printing in this way, using cut wood blocks, is still a flourishing business in India and Persia and the famous 19th-century textile prints of William Morris were also made using this method.

To print by stamping you will need the same equipment as for paper printing, i.e. a roller and slab, white spirit or turpentine and rags for cleaning up and a palette knife or old dinner knife for mixing colours. Place the fabric on a work table, roll up the linoleum with a generous coating of ink, place it face down on the fabric and press carefully and firmly all over the back. Then gently peel the linoleum away from the fabric. To mount the lino block, glue it with PVA adhesive to a block of wood the same as the linoleum and at least 9cm ($\frac{3}{4}$in) thick.

For your working surface use an old blanket stretched over a table, and pin a piece of cotton or polythene sheeting on top. The blanket gives a springy printing surface, and the article or pattern pieces you are printing can be pinned to the backing which can be changed

*Repeat printing of a simple linocut motif (above) has been used to produce the set of table linen shown on the left. The motif is illustrated full size and can easily be transferred onto a linoleum block. The pattern is also ideal for printing the hem of a dress or smock.*

when necessary. Pin the fabric all around the edges, stretched as flat as possible, to keep them from lifting while the block is being moved to the next position. If you are printing a motif which has a correct way up, it is helpful to mark the back of your block with an arrow at the top.

Print by positioning the block on the cloth and then striking it with a mallet or stick. If the block is a small one then one tap will be sufficient but larger surfaces may need several raps. The wood backing spreads the pressure of the blow and guarantees a clear print. An unmounted block would have a darker area of colour at the point you hit it.

## Using fabric dyes

Fabric dyes, even in paste form, are more liquid than inks so it is necessary to give the linoleum an absorbent surface. This is done by a process known as flocking which involves the use of special powdered fibres and a flocking mordant or glue to make it stick. Both are available from art suppliers along with fabric dyes.

Put some flocking powder into a jar and make a number of small holes in the lid or use a salt shaker. Roll the flocking mordant onto a linoleum block that has been cut and mounted on wood. You can use your clean printing roller for this purpose, rolling on the mordant just as you would the colour. If the glue is water-soluble, the roller can be cleaned with water and detergent. Otherwise use the solvent indicated by the manufacturer for cleaning. Sprinkle the flocking powder liberally onto the sticky mordanted surface of the block to make a thick velvet layer. Shake off the surplus powder and repeat the process three times. Leave to dry overnight and then brush off any surplus powder with a stiff brush. Your printing block is now absorbent enough to hold the dye.

To print, first put a blanket underneath the cloth as described. Make a stamping pad by soaking either a pad of fabric or a thin sponge cloth in a dish of dye. Press the block into the pad and then onto the fabric you wish to print. When the block is in place on the fabric strike it with a wooden mallet or stick. Always use the stamping pad to collect fresh dye before each printing. When printing is completed, clean the block with water. If the brand of mordant you are using is not water-soluble then you can re-use the flocked printing block. Otherwise you will have to re-flock in order to print more later. If you wish to remove the flocking powder from the block, and the mordant is not water-soluble, then use the solvent recommended by the manufacturers. Dye manufacturers give instructions for fixing dyes on the fabric, usually by ironing the back of the printed area for five minutes with a fairly hot iron.

*This elegant caftan in apricot silk is entirely hand-printed with linoleum blocks.*

# Several colours on one block

Linocuts can be successfully printed in more than one colour but you must either re-cut your block for each different colour or cut a series of separate blocks. Multi-coloured printing is not as laborious or as complicated as it sounds but you must think out your colourscheme beforehand. When using one block, more and more areas recede, leaving only the areas which still need colouring.

*The house and garden picture described in this chapter was printed in three different colours, a little more of the block being cut away after each printing. By the time that red, the final colour, was printed, little of the surface of the block remained intact.*

93

Right: Mounted and framed the finished linocut makes a very attractive picture. The colours can be varied according to personal choice; here black is used instead of green as the second colour.

Right: Mounted and framed the finished linocut makes a very attractive picture. The colours can be varied according to personal choice; here black is used instead of green as the second colour.

*Opposite: The trace pattern for the house and garden linocut – circles near the fence indicate cuts for daisies. The path should be pebbled by making short gouges. Although the sketch appears to be back to front, it will print the right way round.*

## The house and garden print

The picture of the house and garden is printed from one piece of linoleum cut away in three stages for three successive colours. By cutting the design in stages from the trace pattern you will begin to get a sense of multi-colour printing in lino.

First cut a rectangle of linoleum to size, 21cm by 15.5cm (8¼in by 6in) and trace the pattern (fig.1) onto it using a sheet of carbon paper and a hard pencil. Remember that the tracing pattern is the reverse of the printed design since it is a mirror-image of the block. This is an important point to remember if you have any lettering to do. When you have traced the design, go over all the lines with water-proof black Indian ink. This makes the design clearer and – more important – it will not be washed off when you clean the block.

1.

## First colour

Start cutting by removing all the areas which will remain white throughout. The clouds are outlined with a V-shaped tool and then removed with the larger U-shaped gouge. The roof ridge is cut with the small U gouge. The raindrops, the lines of brickwork, the stone trim and the fence are all cut away with the two V cutters while the daisies are made by removing small V-shaped nicks. The pebbles on the path are cut with the small U gouge. When you have finished cutting the block, cut all the paper you will need, making it a bit larger than the block so you will have a border. You should make as many prints of this stage as you need plus a few others to cover any mistakes. This stage is printed in blue ink as shown in fig.2.

## Second colour

While the blue prints are drying, proceed with stage two of the cutting after cleaning the surface of the linoleum. This stage will be printed in green and the further cuts you have to make are shown in fig.3. All the sky except the rainbow must be removed with a large U gouge. The window panes must also be completely gouged out and a cross cut made in the doorway to make a panel. The roof tiles are outlined and the pebbles are enlarged with a small U gouge.

First make a print of the green stage by itself so you can check your work and also provide yourself with a masking device. When you have a large area of open cutting such as the sky on a linoleum block, the roller tends to dip down into it and deposit a little ink. To avoid accidentally printing the area you need to mask it. In this case you can do it by cutting out the white area of the sky from your green proof (just roughly around the house and trees, leaving a hole for the rainbow). Then lay a blue print face up on the table and fit the cut-out sky over the same area on this print to protect it from possible damage. Ink up the block in green again and gently lower it onto the blue print starting at one edge as if you were closing a book.

## Third colour

The third and final stage of cutting is shown in fig.4. Not very much is left. Further U-shaped gouging with the small gouge has been done on the path and the tree has suddenly produced apples by the same means. The red used to print this stage is mixed with a little brown by blending the two colours together with a palette knife on the side of the inking slab and then spreading the mixture out to be rolled. Never try to mix the colours with a roller. When the final stage is printed (fig.5) you will have a 'limited edition' of hand-cut prints in three colours.

---

**House and garden print**

**You will need :**
Gouges – a small and a medium V-shaped cutter and a small and fairly large U-shaped one.
Black Indian ink.
Craft knife such as a Stanley knife.
Printing roller and slab.
Printing paper such as cartridge paper.
Printing inks in blue, green, red and brown. (Turpentine if they are oil-based.)
Palette knife or old dinner knife for mixing.
Printing press or burnishing tool such as a spoon.
Linoleum block at least 21cm by 15.5cm (8¼in by 6in).
Carbon paper and hard pencil for tracing.

*Opposite: Before each of the three different printing stages (figs.2–4), increasing amounts of the design are cut away from the block. Fig.5 shows the finished print in full colour.*

96

# One block for each colour

The elements to exploit in linoleum printing are those which are peculiar to the medium – a somewhat brash quality and a simplicity of line and colour. Therefore, you should either look for inspiration in designs and patterns that contain these qualities already or adapt existing ones to suit by reworking them in a bolder style.

## Choosing colours

Whether you choose to work with printing watercolours or oil-bound inks depends somewhat on the effect you want. Printing watercolours have a slightly velvety quality all their own and the flower print was made with them. Oil-bound inks offer greater versatility because they are, in some cases transparent and can therefore be over-printed effectively. Different colours of inks and even different brands of the same colour vary in degrees of transparency and covering power. Printing one colour over another may cause them to change, blue over yellow may become green, for example. Therefore, when you are planning your colour scheme it is always wise to try any colours that will be overprinted by making a dab on paper and then dabbing it with the second colour when dry. A special medium called extender, will increase the lightness and transparency of oil-bound inks (adding white will lighten them too, of course). When using extender (or white) squeeze it out first and then gradually add the colour to it. This way you will arrive at the correct shade more quickly and with less waste.

## Printing from separate blocks

Although the print of the house and garden was made by cutting away more and more of the same block for each different colour, a more versatile way of making a multi-coloured print is to cut a different block for each colour. This way you can continue to make prints indefinitely since the blocks are not altered at each stage. When printing in more than one colour you must always figure out before you begin what will be on each block. This is easier to do than it seems and can be simply worked out on preliminary sketches. Sketch your complete design in colour, then using sheets

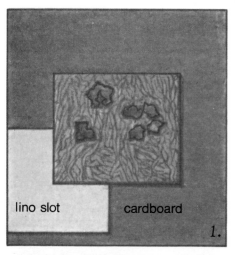

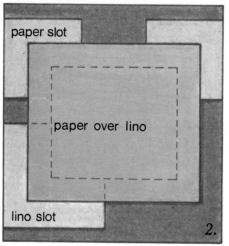

*1. To simplify the lining up of the blocks, attach an L-shaped holder to a wooden baseboard.*
*2. Further L-shaped markers at the top of the board hold the sheet of paper in place.*

of thin tracing paper overlay them one at a time onto the design and make up a different sheet for each colour. The information on each sheet can then be transferred to a separate linoleum block.

When cutting more than one block you can also transfer the design by the offset method. This means cutting the block with the most information on it first and printing it in black onto a sheet of paper. Then, while the ink is still wet, print the wet paper onto one of the other blocks, making sure to line up the edges of the print accurately with the edges of the new block of linoleum. This will give you the information on block number two that is engraved on block number one. You can then either trace the additional information you need or cut the areas freehand. If there is a third or a fourth colour these can be treated in the same way, by transferring the information from the previous blocks.

## Lining up

In the case of the house and garden print previously described, the print registration (fitting of the different colours together on the print) was done by lining up the edges of the second block with the edges of the first colour print but for more advanced work the following method is recommended.

Use stiff cardboard, hardboard or Masonite as a base or backing. Cut out an accurate, right-angled, L-shaped piece and stick this to the lower left hand corner of the baseboard. This card must not be thicker than your lino. The inked blocks will be placed one at a time in this corner and the paper lowered over them to print

*Two possible versions, in alternative colour schemes, of a linocut design suitable for printing from three separate blocks. The design is shown in its component parts overleaf.*

A third possible colourscheme for the flower design is shown here divided into its component parts. The information on each of the three blocks is shown both individually and in combination in the finished flower pattern print (bottom right).

(fig.1). (When printing from more than one block it does not matter in which order you print. But it is most important that each block is aligned properly). Now cut smaller L-shapes for the paper. Since the paper is always somewhat larger than the block you must have a different guide to slot the paper in. Decide where the top of the paper will come to, then stick the L-shapes into place (fig.2). The paper can then be lowered from this position each time you print and you can be assured of its falling into the correct position.

# Screen printing

# Equipment for screen printing

Of all printing methods, screening or serigraphy is the most versatile. It is used on paper for posters, pictorial prints and wallpapers, on fabrics for both dresses and furnishings, on wood, plastics, glass, metal and ceramics. At the same time it is one of the simplest ways of printing and impressive results can be achieved at home. Basically silk-screen printing is a super-efficient stencilling process. The stencil is put beneath or on a meshed fabric that has been stretched across a frame. (The mesh rests on the surface about to be printed.) By pulling an implement called a squeegee across the top of the mesh, ink is forced through it onto the printing surface below in all areas except those blocked by the stencil. This makes the print. This action is quick and simple so that once the equipment is assembled a number of prints can be made much more quickly than with ordinary stencils.

## Development of screen printing

Stencils can be rather complex affairs with several parts held together by fine 'bridges' that inevitably show up on the final print. Furthermore, it is time consuming to lay them out correctly for each printing, especially if they are in several sections. In the 18th century, Japanese stencil cutters began to use hairs to connect the different sections of a stencil since these left only the finest lines on the print. They subsequently evolved a more elaborate system of attaching stencils to a grid of fine hairs stretched across a frame. In the mid-19th century this grid was replaced by silk and silk-screen printing was the result. Nowadays, silk-screen printing is a highly mechanized process. It is one of the most prevalent ways of decorating manufactured cloth and several types of stencil have been developed, including complex photographic ones. But no matter what type of stencil or surface is used, the basic printing process remains the same.

## Equipment

Although the equipment used in screen printing seems complicated at first glance it is really very simple and once the essential items are

---

**The screen**

**You will need :**
4 lengths of 40mm by 40mm (1½in by 1½in) planed, straight-grained, knot-free wood; 2 pieces 25cm (10in) long and 2 pieces 38cm (15in) long.
Panel pins or box nails.
Waterproof glue.
50cm (1ft 6in) terylene screen fabric.
Staples and staple gun or drawing pins (thumb tacks) for attaching the fabric.
Hammer, sandpaper.

at hand they can be used again and again to make prints on all sorts of surfaces using different kinds of stencils and inks.

The basic equipment consists of a screen, i.e. a wooden frame with meshed material stretched across it, a squeegee, printing colours and the stencil. Screen-printing kits containing all these elements are on the market and you can assemble them at home. If you intend to do a lot of printing then it is advisable to make your own screen and squeegee, but if you do buy them choose a size big enough to accommodate a variety of designs.

## To make a screen

The screen is a sturdy rectangle of wood with a meshed fabric stretched across it. It must be larger than the design you wish to print and can be made to any dimensions, but 33cm by 38cm (13in by 15in) is a useful size for repeated use of different motifs. To make the frame, glue and then nail the wood together with panel pins [box nails] to make a rectangle (fig.1). Any unevenness must be planed off as the screen should lie flat on the base. Smooth off the edges with sandpaper.

*Screen printing is a fast way of printing with stencils. If you pull ink across a mesh-covered screen with a 'squeegee' the areas of the printing material beneath which are not covered by the stencil will be printed.*

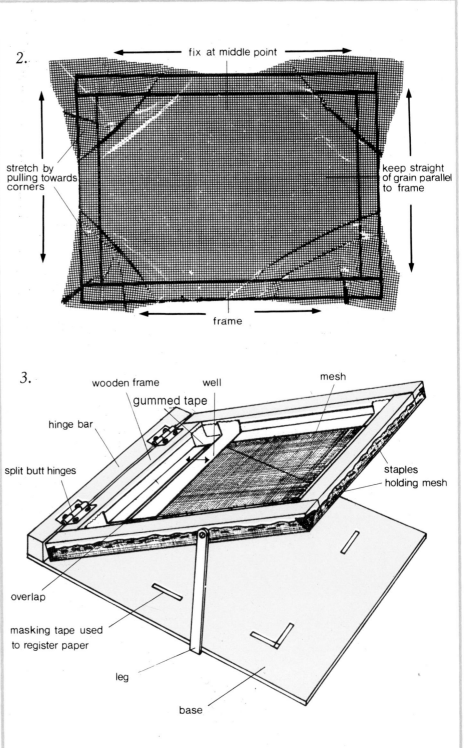

2.

fix at middle point

stretch by
pulling towards
corners

keep straight
of grain parallel
to frame

frame

3.

wooden frame    well    mesh

gummed tape

hinge bar

split butt hinges

staples
holding mesh

overlap

masking tape used
to register paper

leg

base

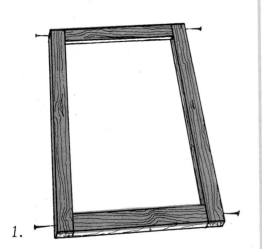

1.

1. A basic screen-printing frame
consists of four pieces of wood
nailed together.

2. To make a screen, meshed
fabric is stretched across the
frame and pinned to it.
3. For printing on sheets of
paper a baseboard is
recommended. It helps position
each sheet correctly and provides
a flat printing surface.

104

Terylene screen fabric is recommended for stretching over the screen frame as it is tough and long lasting. Special terylene mesh can be bought in different gauges from screen-printing suppliers and a medium gauge is recommended for general-purpose printing for beginners. Cotton organdie is often used but has the disadvantage of tearing rather easily while nylon has the drawback of sagging when wet. Silk is ideal but expensive.

To stretch the fabric over the screen cut it to a size 5cm (2in) larger all round than your frame. Using a staple gun tack the fabric to the frame at the centre points on each side (fig.2). Make a double turning along the fabric edges to give more strength and be sure that the mesh is pulled tightly and that the fabric grain is straight. Use your wooden frame as a guide. Continue to stretch and tack down the fabric along the edges working from the centre points outward. Corners should be neatly turned and tacked down.

## The baseboard and hinge bar

The material to be printed must rest on a flat, smooth base, and for printing on sheets of paper it is advisable to make a baseboard which can be attached to the screen frame (fig.3). Nail the length of wood to one 33cm (13in) end of the base (fig.3). Lay one short edge of the frame alongside the bar. Place the opened hinges in position as shown in fig.3 and screw in place. Insert the hinge pins to hold hinges together. These can be easily removed when the screen needs to be taken apart for cleaning. A 'leg' (fig.3) screwed into the side of the frame, so that the screen stands up firmly on its own, is a useful addition.

## Taping

To prevent ink seeping through the corners of the frame apply gummed paper tape to both the outside edges and the inside ones. On the inside edges fold the tape to fit along the upright side of the wooden frame as well as the flat surface of the fabric. It is advisable to apply a second strip overlapping the first strip at the top as shown (fig.3) to make a 'well' for the ink. As the tape dries it shrinks slightly and so stretches the screen even more tightly. If the tape is to be preserved through several washes it will be necessary to seal it with a coat of varnish.

## Squeegee

This is the instrument used to pull the ink across the screen, forcing it through the mesh onto the printing surface. The squeegee consists of a length of doorstop rubber or rubber belting screwed between two pieces of wood with a longer bar glued and nailed

| The screen base |
| --- |
| **You will need :**<br>A piece of 40mm by 40mm (1½in by 1½in) planed wood, 33cm (13in) long.<br>2 sets of detachable butt hinges with removable pins and of a size to fit on wood frame as shown. Screws to attach hinges.<br>Base of plywood, chipboard, blockboard or Masonite 33cm by 38cm (13in by 15in).<br>Perforated metal 'leg' or hinge bar about 30cm (12in) long and washer and screw. |

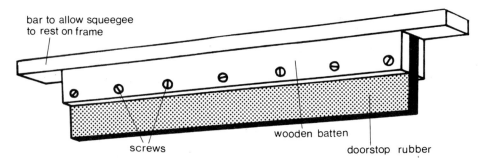

bar to allow squeegee
to rest on frame

wooden batten

screws

doorstop rubber

**The squeegee**

**You will need:**
25cm (10in) length of doorstop
rubber. Two pieces of planed wood,
each 25cm (10in) by 20mm (⅞in) by
10mm (⅜in).
One piece of wood 35cm (14in) by
20mm (⅞in) by 10mm (⅜in).
Panel pins or box nails, screws,
waterproof glue.
Lay the length of rubber between
the two shorter lengths of wood
and screw the three thicknesses
together (fig.4). Glue the longer bar
to the top of the squeegee as shown.

across the top to allow the squeegee to rest in the frame when not in
use. It should be 2.5cm (1in) narrower than the frame (fig.4).

## Printing colours

The colour used for screen printing must be of the consistency of
thick cream, and while pigments suspended in binders of several
kinds can be used, special oil-based screen-printing inks are best for
paper. Fabric dyes in paste form can be used on paper and cloth but
on paper they are not waterproof so they would be unsuitable for
something like a poster. Special inks and dyes are available from
screen-printing suppliers and from some art supply shops. You will
also need turpentine for cleaning up and mixing oil-based inks.

## Stencils

The paper stencil is the easiest way of making a screen print. Use a
thin paper – newsprint is quite suitable – and cut a sheet the same
size as your screen. Draw your design, which can be of quite simple
shapes, and transfer it onto the newsprint with carbon paper. Cut it
out with a sharp craft knife or scissors, depending upon the type of
design and paper used. This is a traditional stencil. The sections
which are removed will print. However, an advantage over stencilling is that with a screen isolated areas do not need 'bridges'. The
screen holds them in place.
Special coated papers are available which make stencils capable of
standing up to very hard use. 'Profilm' is widely used in the United
Kingdom, whereas liquid-adhering film is generally more common
in the United States. Profilm is not waterproof and must be specially
treated for use with fabric dyes and water-based printing inks.
Profilm consists, in effect, of two sheets of paper stuck together – a
backing paper and a glossy film.

## Printing on paper

The cat motif is easy to cut out and is a good stencil to make as you
learn how to screen print. By employing it to make a number of
prints – greeting cards, for example – you will soon see the advantages of this medium over ordinary stencilling.

Cut your stencil as described above from a sheet of paper the size of the screen. Tape the outer edges of the stencil to the frame with a small piece of masking tape on each side. The screen will normally hold the stencil in place by pressing it against the printing surface and the ink will secure it further, but it is wise to secure it to prevent accidents. The separate centre section can be attached to your screen with a dab of all-purpose glue. Next, arrange a place for your wet prints to dry. A line across the room with clothes pegs (pins) to hold the prints is perfectly suitable. Cut your printing paper to size, allowing a margin all round. You can use coloured or white paper as you prefer.

To determine the position of the print on the paper, centre your original trace pattern (or drawing) on a sheet of printing paper. Place this on the baseboard and line it up with the cut stencil by

*Above: Full-size trace pattern for cat motif*

*Left: Screen-printed designs add a distinctive touch to your personal notepaper.*

107

looking through the screen as already described. The drawing covers the area which will print. To make sure the printing paper is always in the correct place you must make some little registration guides. To do this, stick strips of masking tape to the baseboard alongside the edges of the first sheet; these will guarantee correct placement for subsequent prints.

If you are using screen-printing inks you must first thin some colour in a jar by adding a little turpentine to give the consistency of thick cream. (Paste dyes need no additives.) Slide a piece of paper into position. Lower the screen onto it and place the squeegee at the hinged or 'well' end of the screen 2.5cm (1in) or so away from the end wall.

Pour a line of ink into the channel between the wall and the squeegee. You will need to be quite liberal with the ink but after printing unused ink can be returned to the container. With the hinged end of the screen away from you, hold the squeegee in both hands and put it against the edge (fig.5) so all the ink is ready to be pulled towards you. Slope the squeegee a little towards you and pull it firmly right to the opposite end of the screen.

Now, scoop up any remaining ink with the squeegee and carry it back to the top of the screen. Lean the squeegee away from you. The handle will support it against the sides of the screen. Raise the screen to the side prop, pull out your print and hang it up to dry. Repeat the process with the next printing and continue until you have sufficient prints.

## Cleaning up

To clean the inked screen when printing is finished, put some newspapers under the screen. Scrape out any extra ink with a palette knife or old table knife and store it for future use. Tear off the paper stencil and throw it away. Then pour some turpentine onto the screen and clean thoroughly with a rag. Rub well on both sides and keep renewing both rag and newspapers. It does not matter if the mesh of the screen has been stained by the printing colour but it is essential to get the screen completely clear. Check this by holding it up against the light. If the screen is left blocked it will be unsuitable for future work. Make sure all the ink is removed from the corners of the frame too. Don't forget to clean the squeegee and the knife.

If you have been printing with dye, the cleaning-up procedure is slightly different. Take the screen off the baseboard and tear off the paper stencil. Scrape out any dye left over. Run cold water onto the screen and clean it inside and out with a sponge. Give it a good wash with detergent and warm water. Wash the squeegee and the knife.

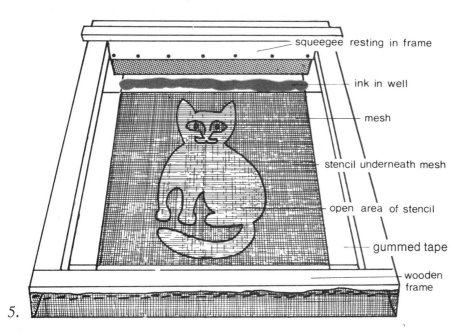

squeegee resting in frame

ink in well

mesh

stencil underneath mesh

open area of stencil

gummed tape

wooden frame

5.

*Paper stencil cut-outs can make very decorative prints, as in this flower-vase design, used on the cover of a scrap book. The zig-zag border was cut with pinking shears.*

109

# Screen printing on cloth

Because of the ease with which motifs can be repeated by screen printing, the technique has become one of the most popular means of decorating cloth, both in the home and industrially. This section deals with simple applications of fabric screen printing – making borders and decorating small areas of garments and household linen, while all-over, repeated patterns and multi-coloured printing on lengths of cloth (and paper) are discussed later.

## Colour

Cloth is printed with dyes and fabric-printing colours, many made specially for screen printing. Colours often require special thickening agents to give them the right consistency. When buying colours for fabric screen printing, always make this clear to the supplier so that any necessary additives can be provided.

## Preparing the work surface

Printing on fabric is very similar to printing on paper but you must use a specially prepared work table (fig.1) and dispense with the wooden base used for printing paper. Spread an old blanket across the table you will be working on and tack or tape it down underneath the table so it is taut. It is important that the printing surface is flat. To protect the blanket, stretch polythene sheeting over it and secure this as well. Make sure your fabric is well ironed and then fix it on top, either by taping it down or with pins. If pins are used cover them with tape to protect the screen.

## Printing a border on fabric

For your first fabric print try using a paper stencil of the peacock motif shown. You can print a single motif or, better still, make a row of peacocks and then make the fabric up into a garment. You can also print the peacocks as a border on a table cloth. Prepare the stencil as for printing on paper. The action of pulling the ink across the screen should hold the stencil in position but the eye of the peacock and the 'eyes' of the tail can be more safely held in place by sticking them to the mesh with a dab of household glue.

*Combined with a mirror image of itself, the above motif can be used as a trace pattern for the design printed on two of the smocks shown opposite. Printing a border can be very much speeded up if a row of motifs is set up on the screen.*

Work out the spacing you want on the fabric by cutting out your trace pattern and marking its position with tailor's chalk on the cloth. If several peacocks are to be printed in a row make a chalk line across the fabric as a guideline for the bottom edge of the

*A number of smock designs have been produced from only two basic motifs by varying colour and using different layouts.*

screen and mark the position of each peacock on it so they will print in a straight line.

It is advisable to ask someone to hold the screen frame down while you squeegee, or you can clamp the frame to the printing table with clamps as shown in fig.1. Print a trial print first on a spare piece of fabric to see if one or two strokes are needed. Absorption varies, and some fabrics need a double application of the dye. After printing the first image, lift the screen by raising one edge first as though it were attached to the base. This will prevent smudging. If you are printing on a T-shirt or other made-up garment, insert card or paper between the layers of fabric to keep the dye from seeping through to the other side.

When printing a repeating pattern such as the peacock on fabric, don't put any part of the screen down on top of the first print unless you are sure it is absolutely dry. Otherwise the dye may off-print onto the screen and smudge the cloth at the next printing. To prevent this, and to avoid having to wait for each motif to dry before continuing, allow the first print to dry for a minute and then cover it with a piece of paper before continuing with the next one alongside it.

To dry the printed cloth hang it up using a double line (fig.2), if it is a sizeable length. When it is dry fix the dye according to manufacturers' instructions. This usually means ironing the fabric on the wrong side.

## Shellac stencils

The disadvantage of paper stencils is that they disintegrate fairly quickly by continual saturation with ink. Shellac stencils, on the other hand, are long-lasting and give a fine, sharp print. Furthermore, they are often easier to make since they are painted and so curved designs and more intricate shapes, which would be difficult to cut out in paper, can be quickly made. Gloss paint and most varnishes can also be used for making stencils for fabric printing but these are not recommended for printing on materials with oil-based inks since these often need thinning with turpentine which might loosen the stencil. (The solvent for shellac is methylated spirit.) Shellac, like paint and varnish, can be bought in hardware stores.

Shellac and paint or varnish stencils are made by painting all the areas of the mesh screen that are not part of the design; in other words turning the mesh screen into a stencil by painting those parts that would have been covered by a paper stencil. The painted areas dry to a hard finish, blocking the 'pores' of the mesh and preventing the dye from penetrating to the printing surface below.

*Trace pattern for the other two smocks on the previous page*

112

With the mesh stretched taut on the frame, place your design in position under the screen and sketch the outline onto the mesh with a soft pencil. Then turn the screen over and, working over newspapers, paint two coats on the outside of the mesh. Cover those areas which are not part of the design. Two coats are necessary to make sure there are no pinholes remaining where ink could penetrate and spoil the fabric below. When it is dry, turn the screen over, prop it up and paint the gummed tape around the inner edge of the frame too. Your screen is now ready to print.

Shellac screens may be cleaned by soaking the screen in methylated

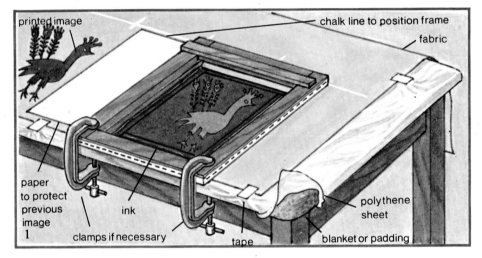

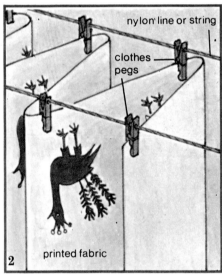

1. A table prepared for screen printing a border on fabric
2. Printed fabric can be hung up to dry using a double line.

*Left: This peacock motif is an easy stencil to cut. It can be traced from the page and enlarged to the desired size.*

spirits and then rubbing it with rags. Then give it a final wash with detergent and warm water and the screen is ready for re-use. Paint and varnish are much more difficult to remove and the screen may easily become damaged in the process.

## Smocks

The children's smocks are printed with shellac stencils as is the mother's. The border for the garments can be used in several different ways as the photograph illustrates. Borders on hem, cuffs or neck-line can all be printed on the cut-out fabric by lining up the design as with the peacock stencil and printing as previously described. Repeat the two trace patterns for the designs across the width of the screen so several motifs will print at once. They could also be used to decorate a table cloth, place mats or sheets and pillowcases.

## Screen printing a tea cosy

Tea made in a pot will be much improved if it is covered with a tea cosy, a traditional part of the English domestic scene. The cotton cloth of the tea cosy and napkin was green to begin with. The border is made by printing the design with blue dye. The rest of the

*Right: Graph pattern of the tea cosy motif shown opposite. To convert it to the correct scale, each square must be expanded to 2.5cm (1in).*

*Below: A tea cosy design of your own can be drawn freehand using these measurements.*

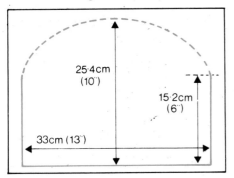

25·4cm (10″)

15·2cm (6″)

33cm (13″)

fabric is printed using a reverse stencil. This means that the areas of the design itself are masked with shellac instead of the background areas. This way the design remains the original colour – in this case green – and the background changes colour.

The tea cosy could be printed in another colour but if you are printing with dyes onto an already coloured cloth bear in mind that they blend. Blue, for example, printed on yellow cloth would become green. If the dye is very thick, as it is on the peacock cloth, this effect can be minimized, however. A less heavy red would have turned orange. Remember also to use either natural fibre cloth, such as linen, cotton, silk or wool, or viscose rayon; synthetic fibre mixture will either not dye at all or will dye as a much paler shade. To make the tea cosy, print the fabric as described. The finished size of the cosy shown is 33cm (13in) by 26cm (10in). Draw a pattern (fig.4) and cut lining 1cm ($\frac{1}{4}$in) smaller than printed fabric. Assemble in the normal way.

*The matching tea cosy and table napkin were designed to blend with the colour scheme of this traditional Mason tea service.*

# Many patterns in many colours

Screen printing becomes considerably wider in its applications when more than one colour is used, and when the technique of printing repeated all-over patterns is combined with multi-coloured printing then the true scope of the craft becomes apparent. Fabric can be produced to match a favourite wallpaper, or wallpaper can be copied onto furnishing fabric. Original designs can be printed for clothing, upholstery and linen to suit your personal taste and to match existing colour schemes.

## Multi-coloured printing

To print more than one colour you need a separate stencil for each colour but this does not mean that you must have more than one screen. You can print the first colour, remove the stencil and clean the screen, then apply the stencil for the next colour. If, however, you plan to do a great deal of screen printing it makes sense to have more than one screen. Figuring out which parts of a design to put on each stencil for multi-coloured printing is comparatively easy. Make your design on paper in the colours in which you wish to print, then trace only those parts which are in the same colour onto the stencils – one for each colour.

When printing in more than one colour you must be able to fit the second stencil over the first printed colour so that it will print exactly the area you want and there are different ways of doing this. When printing more than one colour on single sheets of paper (to make decorative prints for example) you can take advantage of the margin to line up your second stencil correctly for printing. Make two small, butterfly-like triangles in the top and bottom edges of the design and transfer these to the screen stencil (fig.1). The 'butterflies' will then print in the top and bottom margins of the first colour print. By including these registration marks in the stencils of subsequent colours the screen can be lined up properly by positioning it over the first 'butterfly' marks. To align stencils on cloth or other materials where there is no margin it is necessary to use the chalk guides described in the following section.

Overprinting (printing one colour over another) gives varying results

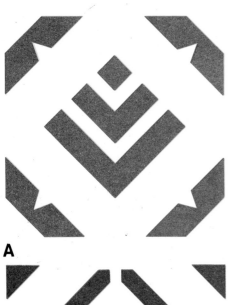

A

B

*Above: Trace patterns for the finished stencil shown opposite. Mark through pin holes to match the corners of stencil B.*

*Above: The completed two-colour pattern. This bold geometric design would be ideal for curtains and bedcovers.*

1. *Corner marks make alignment of the stencil easier.*
2. *Enclose the design motif in a rectangle with intersecting lines at the corners.*

depending on the type of colour you are using, so when designing for multi-coloured printing you must always keep this fact in mind. Screen-printing inks can normally be used either opaque so that they cover exceptionally well or they can be rendered transparent by extender. This gives them something of the quality of dye since the colour underneath is partly visible and effects the final colour. A good way to design for transparent inks is to use bits of coloured tissue paper. By laying one colour over another you can get some idea of the effects of overprinting with transparent inks. Dyes on the other hand tend to blend, and by overprinting, produce a third colour. This can, of course be used to advantage. By using yellow and blue you can make a three-colour design, for instance, since any areas you wish to overprint will be green.

When designing for more than one colour it is wise to avoid butting two solid lines of colour against each other. The slightest imprecision will either result in a dark line of overprinting or a thin white line where the two edges do not quite meet. Commercial printers always try to avoid this situation.

## All-over repeat printing

Repeated patterns on fabric, wallpaper or other surfaces need special planning. The motif must be evenly and successfully spaced, and both the size of the motif and the amount of space between each must be considered. The width of your material to some extent governs the size of your repeat and the number of repeats you can have across the material since the motif must work out evenly across it. Direction is another consideration. Patterns that are one-directional, such as a house design, must of course be printed in an upright position. Since these must be matched up if used on wallpaper, curtains etc., it is worth bearing in mind that a non-directional pattern – one that looks correct from any angle – is more economical.

Repeat designs are worked out on a grid system. First you must draw your motif full-size and enclose it in an accurately-drawn rectangle with each side extended so that it forms a cross at the corner (fig.2). Make sure that the motif is properly centred. This rectangle will provide the basic grid for the repeat. When enclosing the motif you must also decide how much background you want to surround it. Remember that the amount of space within the rectangle will represent half the background between each motif when it is printed.

Since the rectangle will be the total repeat area you must also figure out how many of these will go evenly across the width of the material. For example, a 90cm (36in) wide fabric might have three

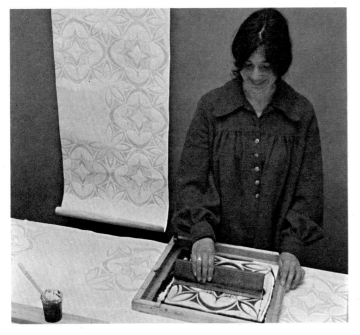

30cm (12in) motif squares or it could have six 15cm (6in) ones – any number that divides evenly. It is advisable to work a section of your repeat by tracing the motif several times on a large sheet of paper to see just what your finished print will look like.

Not all motifs fit neatly into a square yet you must always work within a grid pattern. This means that in some cases part of the motif will extend beyond the lines of the rectangle. But often by having a wiggly line as a pattern edge it is easier to print, since straight lines are more likely to emphasize overprinting or other errors. Irregular motifs can be worked just like regular motifs so that when the rectangles are butted up against each other the design flows continuously.

Once your design is worked out on paper and enclosed in a rectangle of the appropriate size you must make a grid on the material you wish to print which will match up with the design rectangle. First prepare your work table by stretching the material out as described earlier. If you are printing paper you will not need a blanket beneath and you can tape the edge in place with low-tack masking tape. Use as large a work table as possible so that you can print a great deal of the material in one go.

Divide the material on the work table into a grid of rectangles the size of your motif rectangles (fig.3). Use tailor's chalk which will brush off later. Mark the sections with a straight edge or T square. If the material is larger than the table you must wait until you have printed the area on the table before going on to do the next section.

*Above left: Repeat designs are printed in alternate sections to allow the ink to dry.*
*Above: Completing a section of wallpaper by adding the red stage to the final section.*

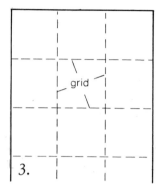

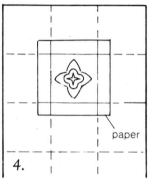

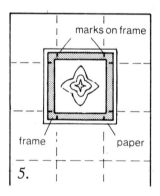

3.

4.

5.

*3. To make an all-over pattern, mark out a grid on the material.*
*4. Key in the corner marks of the original design on the grid.*
*5. Put the screen on the paper and mark where grid lines cross.*

*Right: The finished product: matching wallpaper and curtains*

For wallpaper you can allow for a selvedge which must be trimmed (as with all handblocked wallpapers) or ignore this if you prefer. Often the position of the screen can be marked along the selvedge, however, and the grid is not necessary if the paper is no broader than two screens. For multi-coloured printing you must print the entire material with one colour and then start again if you have only one screen at your disposal. If you have two then you can print the area on the table in the second colour before proceeding to the next length.

Put your original paper design enclosed in a rectangle on the material so that the lines of the rectangle lie on the lines of the chalked grid (fig.4). Lower the screen with the stencil on it so that the screen stencil exactly fits over the design. (If working on cloth, you can tape the paper design to the cloth to steady it.) Then mark with a felt pen on the screen frame the places where the grid lines touch it (fig.5). This will be your positioning guide each time you print. Multi-coloured stencils can be lined up in the same way by positioning the second stencil over the first so that it falls in the right place and the guide-marks can be made.

Remove the paper pattern and you are ready to print. Because it is difficult to see the registration marks on the far side of the screen it is useful to get someone to help you line it up and hold it still while you squeegee. Always print in alternating sections as shown so that recently printed areas have time to dry.

# Photographic screen printing

Photographic stencils are the most versatile and sophisticated of screen-printing stencils. A photographic stencil is one in which the image is developed on light-sensitive material instead of being cut out or painted on mesh in the traditional way. Professional screen printers always use stencils which are made photographically but while they rely on complex laboratory apparatus the process can also be done at home using ordinary household equipment and special, light-sensitive emulsion normally available from screen-printing suppliers.

## The basic process

Photographic stencils are made by coating the screen with light-sensitive emulsion. The design is laid on the coated screen and the screen is then exposed to strong light. The light causes the emulsion to harden in the areas which are not blocked by the design. When the screen is washed in cold water, the emulsion comes off the areas where it has not hardened, leaving the mesh free and making a stencil for printing.

## Photographic screens

Photographic stencils are the most efficient means of making complicated stencils with fine detail. They also have the advantage of being a direct method, something like tusche, since the image itself goes on the screen and not just its outline. Furthermore, all sorts of flat objects – such as feathers, leaves, or lace – which have interesting shapes can be used as designs simply by laying them on the coated screen and exposing it to light. The process sounds difficult because it appears technical, yet it is remarkably straightforward and is highly recommended, particularly for doing a lot of printing. It means you can print not only materials for personal use but original designs for fabrics or wallpaper for sale.

It is very important when making photographic stencils that the design is completely opaque so that no light will penetrate it and cause the emulsion beneath to harden. For this reason, most

---

### A photographic stencil

**You will need:**
Printing screen.
Frosted acetate film such as Kodatrace.
Opaque ink such as photographic retouching ink.
Light-sensitive emulsion.
Length of L-shaped aluminium [aluminum] channel just shorter than the inner width of your printing screen.
Masking tape.
Sheet of clear glass at least as large as your screen.
A board that will fit easily inside your screen.
Piece of old blanket.
Thick, dark cloth.
Sheet of black paper for testing.
Light source.
Clock. Weights.
The acetate film, retouching ink and light-sensitive emulsion are all available from screen-printing suppliers and the retouching ink can also be bought from some art suppliers and from photographic supply houses. Other types of ink can be used so long as they are completely opaque which many inks, such as Indian ink, are not.

designs are painted on a special sheet of film with an opaque ink such as photographic retouching ink. The design to be developed is called a positive.

Acetate film is a frosted, translucent film available from screen-printing suppliers. The film is frosted so that it holds the ink and, because it is translucent, the design can be traced onto it by placing the original drawing underneath the film as a guide. It is also possible to paint the design onto a sheet of glass with opaque ink or put an object such as grass or feathers directly on the coated screen as mentioned previously. As long as the design image is opaque it will act to protect areas of the screen from hardening and so make a stencil. Remember when transferring your design onto acetate or glass that only those areas which are the same colour go on the same stencil. If your design has more than one colour you must prepare a separate positive for each.

## Materials

Light-sensitive emulsion is the key ingredient in photographic stencil making. This is made of potassium dichromate and is best bought already suspended in a gelatin base (otherwise the two must be applied separately to the screen). Exposure to direct, ordinary light makes the emulsion harden and become insoluble so that it cannot be washed off. Some emulsions come in two parts – a 'medium' (solution in which the photo-sensitive agent is suspended) and the photo-sensitive agent itself. When mixed, the solution can be kept a day or two in a dark bottle in a cool place. In addition to liquid emulsions there are photo-film stencils on the market which consist of clear film already coated with emulsion. This type of stencil is not waterproof however and so not suitable for use with fabric dyes or water-based printing inks.

Some photosensitive emulsions are designed for exposure under arc-lights or special ultra-violet lights and these are not suitable for home use unless you buy special lighting equipment. Ultra-violet lights are available from screen-printing suppliers. Do not try to use an ordinary 'suntan' lamp as it will give little success. Always make sure your supplier understands what type of light you will be using. Acetate film, retouching ink and light-sensitive emulsion are all available from screen-printing suppliers and retouching ink can also be bought from some art suppliers and from photographic supply houses. Other types of ink can be used so long as they are completely opaque – which many inks, such as Indian ink, are not. The L-shaped metal channel must be assembled to hold the emulsion and this is done by filing off any sharp edges on the ends and building up a wall at each end with masking tape (fig. 1).

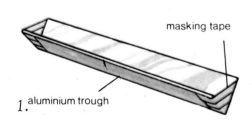

*Improvised metal trough to hold the emulsion*

1. aluminium trough / masking tape

## Coating the screen

Make sure your screen is thoroughly de-greased and dust free before you begin. A washing with detergent and hot water is advisable. When your positive (design image) has been prepared you are ready to coat the screen with the emulsion. Work in subdued light such as a room with the blinds drawn.

Before you coat the entire screen, a test strip should be made to find out the right exposure time for the circumstances. This is done by coating a small section at the bottom of the screen just as you would coat the whole screen (described below) and then exposing this area for different lengths of time as described further on. This need not interfere with the use of the screen later.

Lean the screen up against the wall with the short side horizontal and the outside of the screen facing you (fig.2). Put newspapers beneath it. Fill the trough with emulsion and begin the coating at the bottom of the screen. Press the edge of the trough against the mesh and, tilting it slightly towards the screen, slide it upwards about 5cm (2in) for a test strip and to the top of the screen when preparing for a printing stencil. Applying the emulsion this way is a knack. You should press the trough quite firmly against the mesh as you slide it upwards, otherwise lots of air bubbles form which later burst and turn into pinholes. Deposit as even a layer of the gum-like emulsion as you can. (Practise the motion first with the trough empty.) Then turn the screen around and coat the inside too. Allow the emulsion to dry.

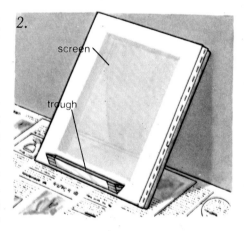

*Coating the screen with light-sensitive emulsion*

## Checking for pinholes

When the screen is thoroughly dry (and this may take several hours) check it for pinholes by holding it up to the light. If there are only one or two these can be 'spotted' with a brush dipped in emulsion. Wash the brush with water to clean. If there are large numbers of pinholes your coating technique is at fault and you will have to coat the screen again.

## Making the exposure

Photo-sensitive emulsion can be exposed by an ordinary light bulb, fluorescent light or direct sunlight. The latter should develop the emulsion in five to ten minutes while several fluorescent 40watt bulbs can be even faster if placed about 20cm (8in) from the screen and about 15cm (6in) apart. A 500watt bulb placed about 45cm (18in) from the screen will develop in about the same time as sunlight, while a 150watt bulb will take at least three hours. However, all these facts vary according to the basic light content in the room and for this reason a test is important and necessary.

Your work table should be placed directly under the light source, but the light must be off. If your source is direct sunlight, keep the blinds drawn. Put one or two books on the table and a board on top of them so that you can place the screen over it like a box lid and the sides of the screen can hang down without touching the table (fig.3). Cover the board with the piece of blanket and place the screen on top of it in the manner just described. If the edges of the blanket make too tight a fit for the screen then you may have to cut the blanket to the size of the board so the screen can fit comfortably over the board which supports the mesh.

Lay the positive on top of the screen mesh. Remember that this is the print side of the screen – the positive must be placed face downward so it will be right way up when the screen is used for printing, otherwise the design will come out back to front. Lay the sheet of glass on top of the positive (unless the positive is painted on glass, or is too bulky). It is a good idea to put some weights on the corners of the glass since good contact between the positive and the screen is essential. Fig.3 shows the layers which are then completely covered by a dark cloth.

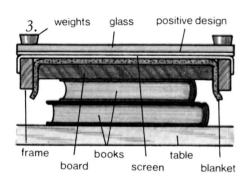

*3. Screen and original ready for exposure to light source*
*4. Test strip used to measure exposure time*

## Exposing a test strip

To make a test of exposure time for the particular environment and light you are using, prepare the screen as described but use for your positive on the coated test strip a zigzag design which will cover the the test strip from top to bottom (fig.4). Have the sheet of black paper in your hand. Expose the test strip to light for two minutes. Then cover one quarter of the strip with the black paper so that three quarters remain exposed for another two minutes. Next slide the black paper along so that half the strip is covered and expose the remaining half for another four minutes.

Slide the paper up leaving only the last quarter of the strip exposed and leave this under the light for a further eight minutes. This means that the quarters will have been exposed for two minutes, four minutes, eight minutes and 16 minutes respectively. Finally, remove the glass and the positive. Take the screen to the sink and run cold water over both sides. Do not rub. (A short length of hosepipe or a hair-washing spray is useful for washing the screen.) Normally the parts of the screen that have been protected from the light will wash away leaving open mesh in those places, but the areas of the test strip will vary and reveal which exposure time is best. On the over-exposed areas the image may not wash out at all, while in the very under-exposed areas everything may wash out.

To expose the whole screen for printing, proceed as for the test strip, but expose the screen only for the amount of time that

*This distinctive motif was printed on a T-shirt using a photographic stencil.*

proved suitable in your test. (The screen may, after washing, be blown dry with a hairdryer.) Then apply gum strip to the edges and the screen is ready to print, using either oil- or water-based inks and dye, depending on the type of material which you are printing on at the time.

## Laboratory stencils

Positives may also be made by preparing a design in black and white on paper (each colour in the design is shown on a separate sheet) and getting it photographed and printed onto transparent film as a positive. Most screen-printing suppliers provide this service.

The advantages of this method are that the artwork (as your drawing is called) may be easily enlarged or reduced. Also, if you are making a screen full of a tiny repeat pattern, such as minute flowers, it can save you hours of work. One repeat unit can be quickly multiplied by photographing several positives on film and these can be assembled to cover the whole screen. When making photographic repeats be sure to make two repeat crosses in the

*Right: Shoulderbag made from screen-printed fabric*

margins of your artwork. This is important for assembling all the repeat units side by side on the screen and when this is done the crosses can be scratched off the film with a sharp blade.

## Strawberries

The strawberry fabric was made using a photographic laboratory to multiply the repeat unit. One complete repeat unit – a rectangle filled with the strawberries as shown – was drawn up as two sheets of artwork, one for each colour. Each was photographed and a number of photographic positives on film were printed. These were then assembled to cover the surface of two screens (one for each colour). The design could also be made by painting in every single strawberry until the screen is covered. Or you could mask out all the screen, except one strawberry, and use this one unit to print motifs on small items such as napkins.

*Below: The repeat unit for the strawberry fabric, enclosed in a rectangle for repeat printing*

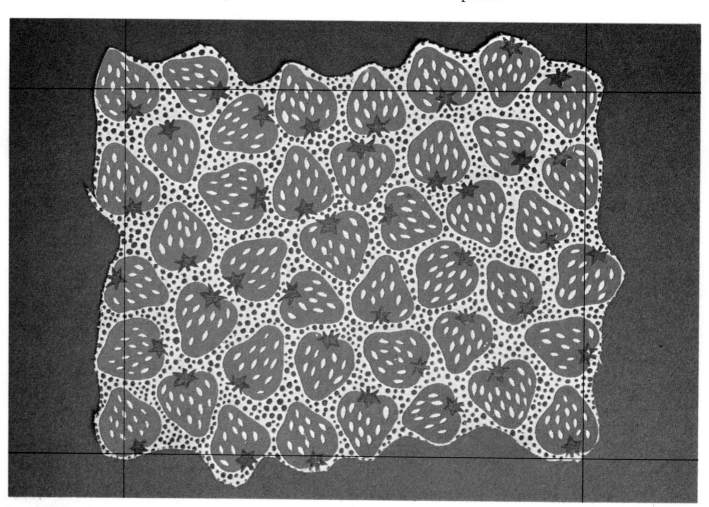

# Screen printing without stencils

Direct-gum screen printing is a method of producing a series of prints without a stencil and from only one screen (normally a separate screen is required for each colour). The complete design is painted directly on the screen with dyes and squeegeed through the mesh with gum which forces the painted design onto the material below. Between six and 12 prints can be made from one application of the dye and these will range from full-strength to pastel shades.

## Uses

Direct-gum printing can be used on paper or on fabric, and although both are printed in the same way, the process is somewhat simpler on paper since fewer chemicals are required to activate the dye. In paper, coverings for boxes, files or books can be produced, or original prints made for framing. Enough fabric can be printed to make a roller blind or a lampshade and cushions – each cushion becoming more subtly toned than the one before it.

## Preparing the screen

Whether you are printing on paper or on fabric, the basic rules apply. Since the design is painted on the screen, bold, flowing lines are more suited to the medium than small geometric patterns, for instance. Designs can be applied free-hand, or a preliminary drawing can be made for transfer onto the screen. A photograph from a magazine could also be used as a guide.

To transfer the design to the screen in colour, place the preliminary drawing or photograph under the screen and prop the screen on all four corners by at least 6mm ($\frac{1}{4}$in) so that it does not touch the design beneath (otherwise the dye will not be applied evenly). Mix the dye according to instructions given here and then paint the design on the screen with dyes. Always allow the dye three or four minutes to dry before applying a second colour beside the first, otherwise they may blend and change colour. The screen can also be placed flat over the design (without props) and the outline of the design sketched lightly on the screen with a pencil. Afterwards, however, the screen must be propped up to apply the dye.

While ordinary cold-water dyes are only suitable for printing on

*In direct-gum screen printing the complete design is painted onto the screen itself. Primary colours are used to good effect on this roller blind and map storage bin. The density of colour varies according to the amount of thickening agent added.*

128

*Opposite: Brighten up your deck chairs with colourful designs on the back. Between six and twelve prints can be made from one application of dye.*

paper using this method, fast-acting cold-water dyes can be used on both paper and fabric. Cotton and viscose rayon are recommended but before use they should be boiled for half an hour, preferably in a little cleansing agent (Lissapol D) and then rinsed thoroughly to remove any chemical finishes or impurities.

## Printing on paper

Prepare the dye and mix in gum thickener according to manu-facturer's instructions. Paint the design on the screen as previously described. Place the screen over the paper to be printed and pour a line of dye thickener in the 'well' of the screen. Then pull the squeegee forward to print. If you are printing a repeat design, never place the screen on any part of a wet print but let it dry first. It is generally easier to space the motifs fairly far apart. As the dye is transferred at each printing, the design on the screen will gradually fade and so will the prints.

## Printing on fabric

This involves mixing dyes and thickener separately. The following gum-thickener basic mixture must be made first. Part of it is used to thicken the dyes for painting on the screen; the remainder is used along with other ingredients to squeegee the design and fix it on the

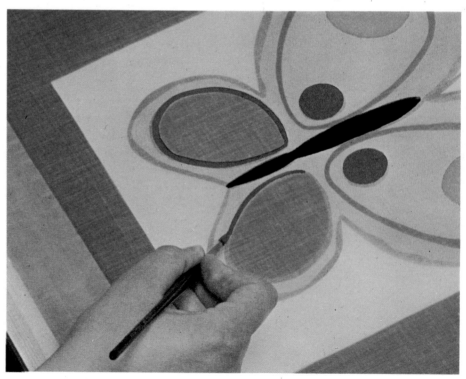

*Right: Tracing a motif directly onto the screen is a relatively simple process. Using this method an unlimited number of colours can be printed at once.*

130

fabric. Dissolve 1 tablespoon of water softener in 170ml (6fl oz) of warm water, sprinkle 4 tablespoons of gum thickener on the mixture and stir for 5 to 10 minutes. Leave the gum to stand overnight and remove any lumps by straining.

Fast-acting cold-water dyes are completely intermixable and a wide range of colours may be obtained from the three primary colours of red, yellow and blue. The higher the ratio of water to dye, the paler the shade. In order to obtain the correct paint-on consistency, these dyes must usually be mixed with gum thickener as well as squeegeed with it to print. Mix the dye according to manufacturer's instructions. This usually involves adding boiling water and allowing it to cool, then adding the soda, salt and urea.

The proportion of dyestuff to thickening agent can vary according to the effect you wish to make, but the maximum ratio of thickening to dye mixture should be 50:50. The design may also be applied without additional thickening but it will run or spread out slightly. This can be used to good effect, however, as illustrated in the blind. The blue waves were applied without thickener, while the yellow, orange and red each had different amounts of thickener mixed in. Unlike the gum thickener used for squeegeeing the design onto paper, chemicals must be added for fabric printing which will react with the dye on the fabric and render it fast. The instructions given are for enough gum to print an average design about a dozen times. Dissolve 10 tablespoons of urea in 256ml (9fl oz) warm water and add four cups of thickener from the amount previously mixed. Next add 1 tablespoon of Resist Salt L and allow mixture to cool thoroughly. Just before proceeding to print add $1\frac{1}{2}$ tablespoons sodium bicarbonate and stir. Print in the same fashion as paper.

When the fabric prints are completely dry they must be fixed by ironing for three minutes per 900sq cm (1sq ft) using the maximum possible heat for the type of fabric. Then rinse the fabric in cold running water to remove any surplus colour. Finally, boil the fabric for 5 minutes in water and a little cleansing agent in order to remove the gum thickener. The colour will now be completely fast. When the printing is completed wash the screen and squeegee very thoroughly in hot water.

## Variations

Even after washing, the design will remain faintly visible on the mesh and may therefore be painted over and over again in order to reproduce more of the same design or to overprint some of the original printings, altering the position somewhat. Since the dye is transparent it will always alter its colour when it comes in contact with the colours previously printed.

---

### Printing on paper and fabric

**You will need:**
Screen ready for printing, and a squeegee.
Selection of brushes for applying colour.
Rubber gloves.
Bowls to contain dyes and gum.
Spoons for mixing.
Fabric or paper for printing.

### Printing on paper

**You will need:**
Cold-water dye in colours of your choice.
Washing soda.
Salt.
Gum.

### Printing on fabric

**You will need:**
Fast-acting cold-water dyes.
Gum dye-thickening agent.
Water softener.
Urea to dissolve the dye.
Special salt such as Resist Salt L.
Cleansing agent.
Baking soda.
Additives for dyeing fabric with fast-acting cold-water dyes are obtainable from craft shops and screen-printing suppliers who sell these dyes.

# Mixed-media printing

A variety of printing techniques has been discussed in the course of this book. Some, such as potato printing, are simple and direct while others, like screen printing, require considerable preparation, yet are more efficient for printing a repeated design.

## Choosing the right technique

Before you begin to print you must first decide which technique will be best for your design. This depends partly on the placement of the design and the amount of repeat printing involved. If you are printing a repeat pattern on a quantity of cloth then you might choose screen printing as your method while a single motif on a pocket would be easier to cut from a potato or lino block and stamp on. There is no reason to confine your efforts to one form of

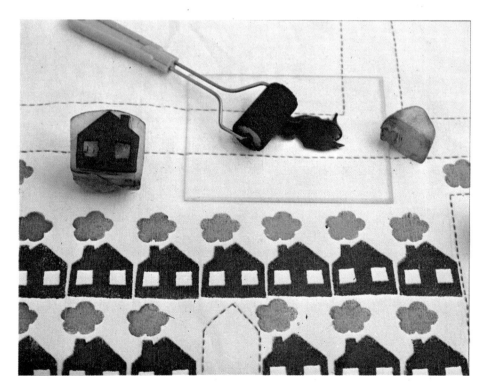

*This attractive house and tree design was printed using a combination of different methods. The two basic motifs were screen printed with a paper stencil but were also cut from potatoes. This gave greater flexibility in filling odd corners of the pattern.*

1. *The house motif is suited to linocut, ordinary stencil, potato or screen printing.*
2. *The tree motif can be stamped on with a potato or screen printed in repeat.*
*Right: Part of the finished product, a matching child's apron and rag doll.*

printing, however, even on one garment. It can be a definite advantage to combine two methods as is shown here.

## House and tree fabric

The clothes and doll patterns shown are printed on a cotton sheet. The outlines of the garments can be drawn in tailor's chalk or with a pencil. The house and tree (figs.1 and 2) were screen printed with a simple paper stencil but both were also cut from potatoes. This way small areas which require very few motifs can be quickly stamped. This also simplifies the special placement necessary on the circular bib.

If you use a screen to print repeats of both the house and the tree motifs then you will need to make a separate stencil for each colour. You might therefore find it more desirable to screen print only the houses and to stamp the trees in place with the potato. To align the motif borders use tailor's chalk and a ruler to make a base line.

*The variety of arrangements possible using the same basic motif is well illustrated by this series of designs for a child's wardrobe, printed on a single cotton sheet.*

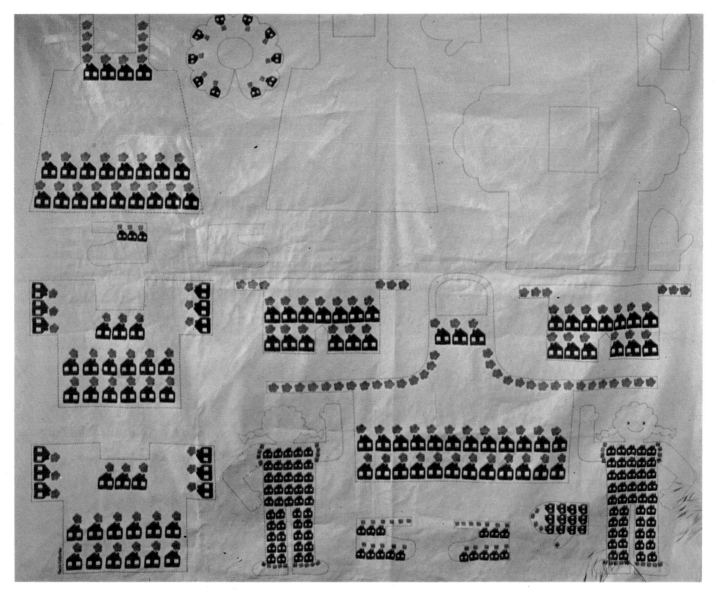

# Index